P9-CJM-442

Railways and War
before 1918

Mechanised Warfare in Color

RAILWAYS
AND WAR
before 1918

by
DENIS BISHOP

and
KEITH DAVIS

THE MACMILLAN COMPANY
NEW YORK, N.Y.

© 1972 Blandford Press Ltd

All rights reserved. No part of this book may be reproduced
or transmitted in any form or by any means, electronic or
mechanical, including photocopying, recording or any
information storage and retrieval system, without permission
in writing from the Publisher.

THE MACMILLAN COMPANY
866 Third Avenue, New York, N.Y. 10022

First published in Great Britain in 1972 by
Blandford Press Ltd., London

Library of Congress Catalog Card Number: 72–78570
First American Edition 1972

Printed in Great Britain

INTRODUCTION

War has always been a matter not merely of fighting but of communication; in the last resort if other things were all equal, the side with the best supplies won. In the 19th century particularly, as mobility improved and rapid-firing weapons became a normal part of every country's armoury, the problem of supply became acute. It was therefore natural that the new-fangled railways should be investigated as a possible means of rapid transport but one is surprised that more notice was not taken earlier. As early as 1838, troops were conveyed by rail in Britain to cope with the notorious Peterloo incident in Manchester, but this remained for many years an isolated incident; it is true that during the British–Russian Crimean War in 1854–55 a limited amount of contractors standard-gauge equipment was sent out and used for local supply but this had no significant effect on the British Army or its quartermaster branch. It might well have declared 'That is not our way of working', the ringing but unprophetic words that Lord Kitchener was to pronounce sixty years later when confronted with the idea of tactical light railways. So, except for stirrings in Prussia, the use of railways in war remained dormant on the European continent. It was, or so they claimed, left to the North Americans to realise their potential in practice.

Certainly the first real attempt to use railways for war purposes was during the American Civil War between 1861 and 1865. Some of the more 'popularised' uses such as the mounting of mortars or bombards on railway trucks were in practice of little importance. The existing railway system did, however, play a large part in supplying the victorious Union armies—and the southern lines contributed indirectly through the use of their rails and sleepers as fortification materials!

Rail supply, too, was a planned feature of the Franco-Prussian War of 1870, at least on the Prussian side, while the French used their system for the evacuation of refugees, a foretaste of things to come.

All these early uses were of the existing systems, however. Perhaps the first attempt at a truly military railway came during the British Egyptian and Sudan campaigns of 1882 when Lord Kitchener, the British Commander in Chief arranged for a substantial amount of railway material to be sent out from England and had laid a standard gauge line to provide a supply route from his base on the Nile. In the event, comparatively little use was made of this link since the campaign was nearly over by the time it was finished, and it was later dismantled.

Its construction and use did, however, set a trend towards more distinctly military use of railways. Perhaps the most famous example is the armoured train that operated so ignominiously on the British side during the South African Boer War at the end of the 19th century and almost caused the death of the future British premier Winston Churchill. Its notoriety quite obscured the fact that, before the war was ended, no less than twenty similar though better armed trains were proving invaluable both in harassing the

Boers and in protecting the many miles of friendly and 'hostile' railways being used to supply the advancing British armies as they laboriously 'cleared' Boer territory. It was this war, too, that gave at least the British most of their early experience in military operations of civilian railways; they not only imposed a degree of military control on the civilian systems in the British provinces but operated the former Netherlands South African Railways as a completely military system. The lessons learnt in speedy ways of repairing demolished lines and bridges were to be of tremendous value later and the right conclusions were drawn by other nations also.

By the end of the war in 1902, the railway branch of the British Royal Engineers was firmly established and two permanent railway companies were kept in being with their own training railway in England. Simultaneously the French organised their 10th Section of military engineers as a railway force, and the Germans increased their already large number of regular and reserve railway engineer companies. It will be noticed that armies were at this time thinking mainly of the problems of operating existing civilian railways under wartime conditions, but they did have an eye also to more directly military concerns. Much less publicised in fact, but just as effective, were the experiments carried out by several of the major European powers to develop military railways, initially for use in their colonies. The Germans, in their very thorough way, had already set up a thriving military railway department after the Franco-Prussian War. In their south-west African colonies in parti-

cular, but at times elsewhere also, they used military railway material and personnel to establish and operate colonial supply links. These lines were largely on the 60 cm gauge designed to be semi-portable and quickly laid and their large-scale operation provided very valuable experience for future design. In addition, at home in Germany, the military railways department of the new German Empire influenced civilian railway construction in many ways to allow easily for future military use. In particular certain 'strategic' lines were built even if potential civilian traffic did not justify them, large junctions were laid out as through-stations on the Prussian model, rather than as dead end-terminals, to facilitate the flow of supplies, and operating methods were slowly standardised so that the whole railway system could be put on a war footing at short notice. Even the locomotives and stock, increasingly standardised for load capacity, were designed with an eye to the necessity for operating over other people's loading gauges; many Prussian locomotive classes, for instance, had their funnels assembled in two parts and bolted together so that their height could quickly be lessened if required. The French did not undertake so many developments, using their 'standard' metre gauge in the colonies and failing to standardise at home on such vital items as coupling design and buffer heights. After the 1870–71 war, they had adopted a defensive posture, building a series of massive fortifications along their eastern frontier and their 'strategic' main-line railways were laid out mainly to service these. Ironically, their fear of attack led them even to break standardisation deliberately in some respects; local railways in the Ardennes area were laid to an 80 cm gauge instead of the metre gauge then standard for such lines, so that an 'enemy' could not easily use them with his own material.

The British, the really great colonial power of the period, compromised as the British usually did. At home, as a result of the South African experience the two 'railway companies' were formed in the Royal Engineers and early in the 20th century a permanent base and standard gauge training railway were established at Longmoor in Hampshire. Little construction of military equipment was undertaken initially, it being envisaged that civilian equipment would be requisitioned in case of need. In the colonies, however, especially in India where communications to the turbulent north and west frontiers were vital, considerable use was made of long narrow gauge railways often designed and controlled by the military. The British military railways department was very influenced by the prevailing theoretical ideas on light railway transport, especially those of E. R. Calthorp, and they consequently adopted a gauge of 2 ft 6 in. (approx. 76 cm) as the most useful compromise between lightness and load-carrying capacity. The Royal Engineers took this work extremely seriously, setting up full scale training lines, first at Chattenden in Kent and then, from 1904 on, at their Longmoor base; a 'complete 2 ft 6 in. gauge equipment', including experimental petrol engined locomotives, was stockpiled in case of need in any future sieges.

As the dangers of war gathered round Europe from 1912 onwards, so the great powers in particular developed and improved their ideas of communication in war. It may be said that only in Europe, and in the European colonies at this period, was there any concerted study of how railways might be used in war. North America, once more united, was comfortably aware of the remoteness of a possible invasion and her armed forces were at a low ebb; most of the smaller countries outside Europe had quite enough problems in opening up civilian communication lines without spending money on military railways.

Yet in Europe the greater powers all developed their railways for war purposes in two ways: the national systems were to some extent organised so that they could be utilised as supply routes for the armies—a procedure most marked in Germany where it turned out that within 48 hours of mobilisation the whole railway machine could be altered to serve the military efficiently. They all developed also, to some extent, the concept of 'field' railways, *feldbahnen* or *chemins de fer militaires*, light, narrow gauge lines that could be laid fairly quickly, if need be over difficult terrain, to serve military front lines.

The position for the major European powers involved in World War One can be summarised briefly. Germany was without doubt the most thoroughly prepared and experienced. She had a large and expert military railways department; the civilian railway personnel, especially the Prussians, were organised largely on military lines and their equipment and railways were easily convertible to military use.

As a result of colonial experience and the foresight of the General Staff in preparing for all eventualities, a large quantity of 60 cm gauge *feldbahn* equipment had been stockpiled and procedures worked out for its deployment and use in the event of a static war developing.

Her main partner Austro-Hungary was less prepared but had for some time been using military railways on the 76 cm gauge in Boznia and Herzegovinia, had standardised on this gauge and its associated equipment details for civilian minor railways, and had stockpiled further equipment for military use. Like the British, but with more reason, they calculated that the new military lines might be long and through difficult terrain so that reasonable load-carrying capacity would be needed.

France, beyond making provision for military control of the civilian railways in time of war, especially in the case of the big *Nord* and *Est* companies, did little in the standard gauge field. Her development of light railways on the 60 cm gauge 'Decauville' pattern, however, was considerable and strongly encouraged by the artillery branch of the army. Extensive permanent systems radiated from all the large fortifications along the Eastern frontier and a certain amount of 'temporary' equipment was stockpiled including stock capable of handling guns even up to 24 cm calibre. Little or nothing was done about standardising the country's metre gauge local railways since by this time the 'doctrine of the offensive' permeated the French army and it was confidently expected that most of any war would be fought on enemy soil!

Britain continued as she had done before, largely unprepared for a large scale land war away from her own soil

but with a nucleus of hard won experience to draw on and an organisation which could be readily expanded in case of need. Field railway material was still confined to the 'complete 2 ft 6 in. gauge equipment' which was, significantly, held by the Siege Parks side of the Royal Engineers.

Of the other powers involved, none was well organised for railway transport. Russia's railways were embryonic and 5 ft gauge at that, Italy was largely unworried and had her own internal problems, Belgium, while having large and standardised networks of both standard and metre gauge lines, intended to remain neutral.

Consequently, when World War One did break out in August, 1914, and when, after only six months it settled down, in the West especially, to a stalemate with the opposing armies facing each other across a line of trenches, it was the Germans who were quickest off the mark. By mid-1915 a complete network of light railways spread out behind their front line, run on proper railway principles. Behind them was all the might and efficiency of the German main line railway system. Next in line were the French and then the British. It must be confessed that the allies on the Western Front had problems not common to their opponents. While the southern half was almost exclusively French, in the north there were Belgians, French and British armies intermingled just as they had been thrown in to stop the German advance. To serve these initially there were only the existing lines of the C.F. du Nord and the C.F. de l'Est—essentially civilian concerns, still having to meet the civilian needs of their areas and now seriously overstrained and under divided military control. At first only French material and personnel were used but these proved insufficient and bit by bit British equipment and personnel appeared, at first to help in operation and then to take over existing routes, to construct and operate new lines. In typically British fashion this rapid expansion of the original two 'Railway Companies R.E.' into the 'Railway Operating Division' was achieved by requisitioning both men and equipment from the civilian railways; it led to a wide variety of locomotives and stock appearing but, given the professionalism of the enlisted personnel, it worked surprisingly well. They were soon supplemented by purpose-designed locomotives and stock and by further railway companies.

In light railways the French, who already had much experience and material, were the first of the allies to realise the importance of such systems to link railhead and front line. Following the supply difficulties experienced by all armies during the appalling winter of 1914–15 they promptly laid networks in rear of most of their army positions and placed large orders for new material, both in Britain and America. Consequently when the British at last woke up to the problem, late in 1915, they found much of their own manufacturing capacity was already fully committed.

The British use of railways provides an interesting study of the national characteristics. Initially caught unprepared, they were able quickly to improvise an effective 'main-line' force to get supplies up to railhead from the Channel ports, and indeed, to construct and organise a very effective cross-Channel ferry service involving a complete new port at Richborough. The stubborn belief of their military commanders that the war would soon become a war of movement inhibited the development of light railway connections from railhead to front line. (Ironically the 'complete 2 ft 6 in. gauge equipment', designed for siege warfare, was shipped off to Egypt almost as soon as virtual siege conditions prevailed on the Western Front.) It was only after individual units in desperation improvised their own tramways—often man-hauled and wooden-railed—that the decision was taken to go ahead with a proper organisation later known as the Light Railway Operating Division (L.R.O.D.). Large quantities of equipment were then ordered, much of it from America owing to the insufficient capacity available in Britain. At first this was sufficient only to equip the areas selected for the next big breakthrough but as offensive after offensive failed to make much headway, a fairly complete, connected system grew up behind the British lines and an informal but extremely effective mode of operation was developed. At their peak, with some 1000 km of line, over 800 steam and 700 petrol locomotives, the British light railways were probably the most extensive and efficient network of forward area communications on either side. It is significant that the only two areas in which the massive German offensives of spring 1918 made any headway were those two areas still comparatively weak in light railway communications. Again it is somewhat ironic that the British had just about perfected the art of supplying a static front when the war exploded into that war of movement they had been expecting for so long and the light railways were rapidly left behind.

Inevitably the events on the Western Front overshadowed events elsewhere and the very scale of the operation meant that most of the railway interest was concentrated there. There were, however, a number of other fronts and new or existing railways played their part in communications on all of them. In the fight against Italy, the Austrians built several long and heavily engineered narrow gauge lines together with many lighter lines and cableways to supply their armies in the mountainous terrain of Sud Tirol, while the Italians made some use of light railway equipment. In the Middle East, an extensive network, of both 2 ft 6 in. and 60 cm gauge supplied the Suez canal defences and isolated lines supplemented the badly damaged Palestinian railways as allied forces advanced in the later stages of the war. In Salonika, Germans, Turks, French and British built extensive feeders, both standard and 60 cm gauge, from the one existing railway to supply their troops on the far ranging and largely static front; these included the only examples—one German, one British—of what might be termed 'strategic' 60 cm gauge railways, properly engineered and running for 50 miles or more over difficult terrain. In Mesopotamia 2 ft 6 in. railways, mainly with material brought from India, played a part and even in Africa light railways were used. Two shaky 60 cm gauge lines helped supply our armies in their attempts to defeat Von Lettow-Worbeck in the east while in German South-West Africa the retreating colonists gained time by tearing up the 60 cm gauge Otavi railway—the only practicable route to the interior. Not until South African engineers had laid in a new line could pursuit be effectively maintained.

With motor transport and aerial bombardment both still in an embryonic stage World War One was undoubtedly the high point of such use and without the railways—in particular the specialised military systems—effective supply would have been difficult if not impossible. Its impact on the development of railway equipment was equally significant particularly in the rapid improvement of internal combustion engined machines, and in the considerable strain it placed on the civilian railway systems.

**American Civil War
Mid-1860s**

1
A Confederate patrol on the line

2
The famous 4-4-0 *The General*

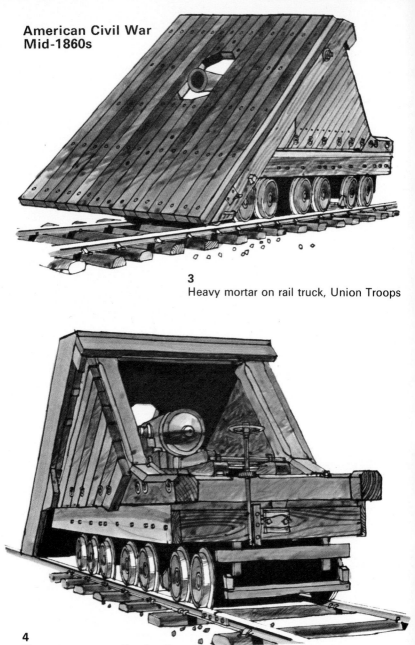

**American Civil War
Mid-1860s**

3
Heavy mortar on rail truck, Union Troops

4
Heavy mortar on rails, showing armour

5
A Prussian troop train blown up when crossing a bridge at
Mezières

6
Zwillinge 0-6-0Ts and auxiliary tender

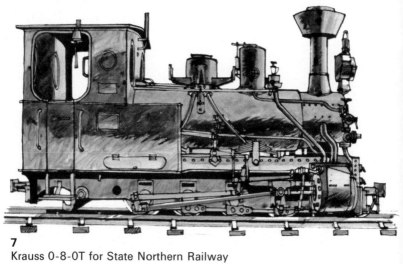

7
Krauss 0-8-0T for State Northern Railway

Jung 0-8-0T for State Northern Railway

German S.W. Africa
1897-1910

9
Klien Lindner method of axle articulation

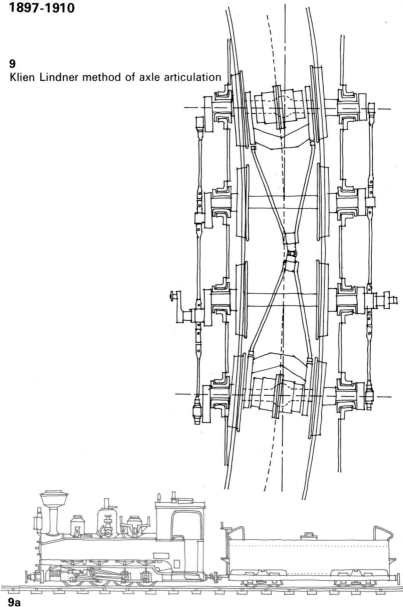

9a
Feldbahn 0-8-0T and auxiliary tender

**German S.W. Africa
1897-1910**

10
Motor inspection trolley (60 cm gauge)

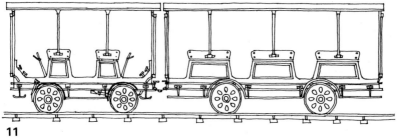

11
30 years later: Drewry inspection car and trailer

12
Restoring rail communications

Military Railway Operating Problems: South African War 1899-1902

South African War
1899-1902

13
No. 18 armoured train and its operating area

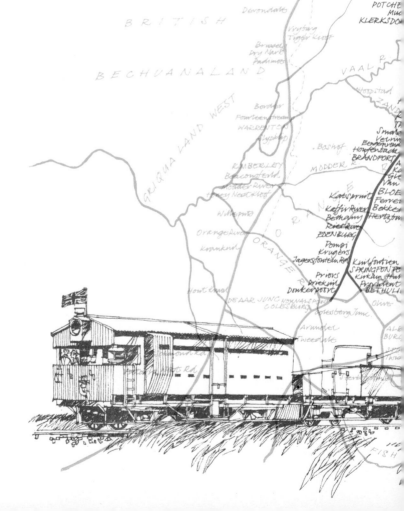

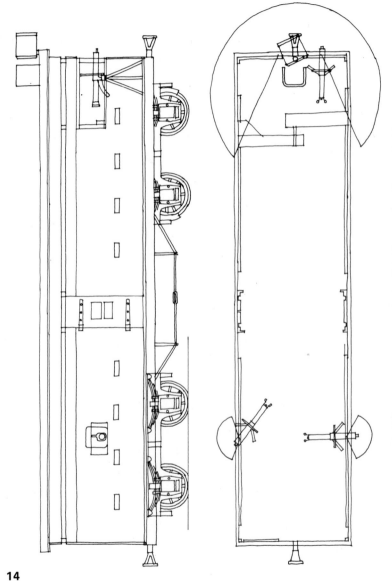

14
Bogie Maxim gun truck, standard pattern

15
Protected bogie truck for supply trains

16
Early pattern 1-pounder gun truck

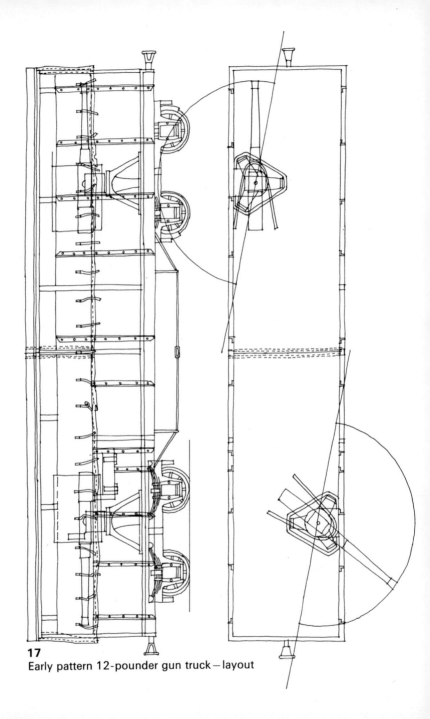

17
Early pattern 12-pounder gun truck — layout

18
Early pattern 12-pounder gun truck

19
Later pattern 12-pounder gun truck

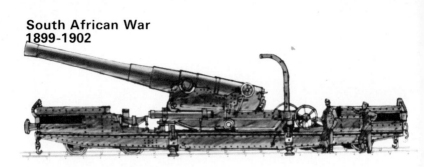

20
9·2 inch gun on experimental rail mounting

21
6 inch gun firing from a railway mounting

22
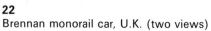
Brennan monorail car, U.K. (two views)

Early 20th-century Experiments

23
Scheil gyro-car, Germany

24
Wolseley-engined petrol tractor, U.K.

25
Belgian locomotive on canal bridge as rebuilt by Royal Engineers

26
Badges of the French military railways

27
Shunting locomotive at Richborough

28
Arrangements for docking train ferry

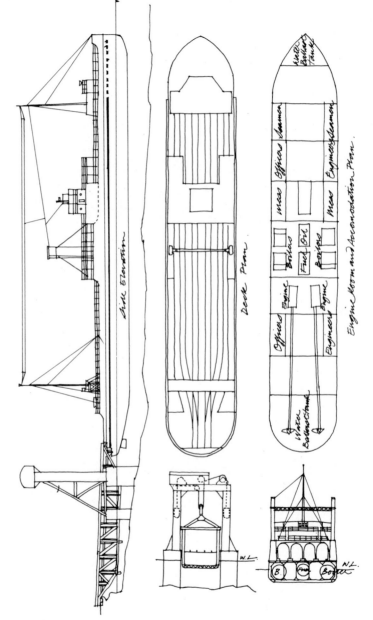

Side Elevation.

Deck Plan.

Engine Room and Accommodation Plan.

Water Ballast Tanks

Officers Seamen

Mess Officers Seamen

Mess Engineers Seamen

Officers Engine

Boilers

Fuel Oil

Boilers

Engineers Engine

Water Ballast Tanks

W.L.

B. Fuel Boilers W.L.

29
The cross-Channel train ferry: layout of ship

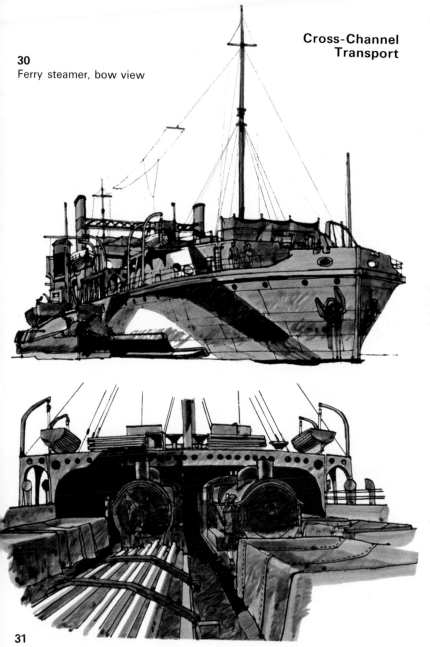

30
Ferry steamer, bow view

31
Ferry steamer, train deck

32
Standard 2-8-0 goods locomotive, U.K.

33
Requisitioned goods locomotive pulling a heavy gun, U.K.

Rail-borne Artillery

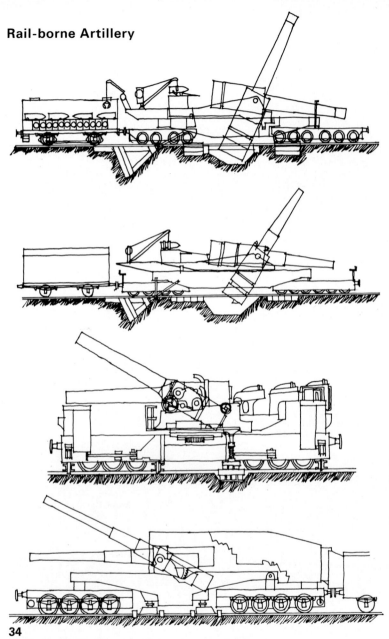

34
Methods of siting heavy rail-borne guns, France

35
370 mm gun on rail mounting, France

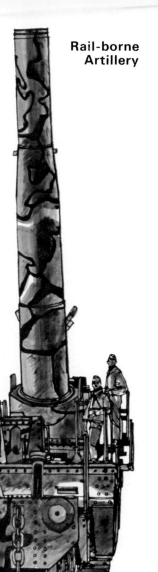

Rail-borne Artillery

36
320 mm rail-borne cannon, France

37
240 mm TR gun on 60 cm gauge trucks, France

38
240 mm gun firing from 60 cm gauge, France

39
12-inch howitzer on rail truck, U.K.

Rail-borne Artillery

40
12-inch Mk IX gun on rail mounting, U.K.

42
30 cm captured railway gun, Germany

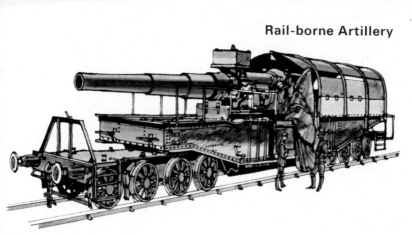

41
28 cm long barrelled gun, Germany

Special V.I.P. Trains
1914-18

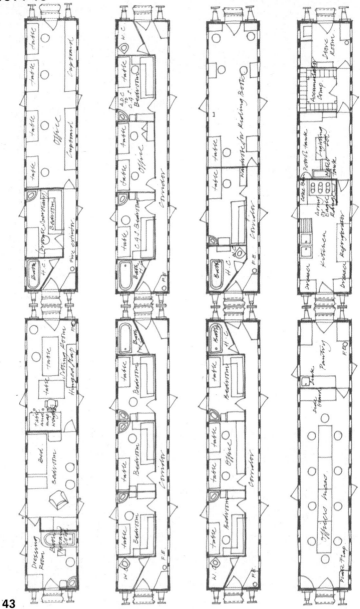

43

Layout of special train for C-in-C, U.K.

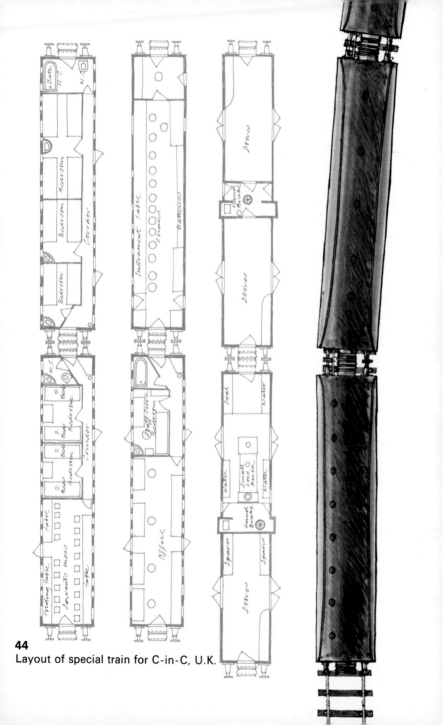

44
Layout of special train for C-in-C, U.K.

Special V.I.P. Trains
1914-18

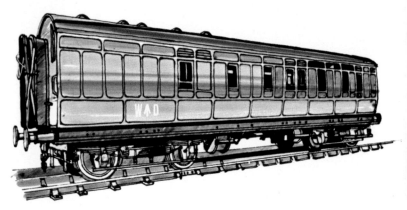

45
Full brake coach in C-in-C's train, U.K.

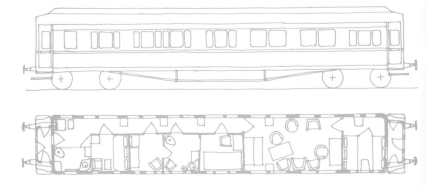

46
Layout of special sleeper for Premier Clemenceau, France

47
10-ton 4-wheeled goods van, U.K.

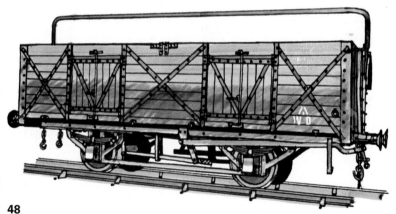

48
20-ton 4-wheeled open wagon, U.K.

Standard Gauge Freight Rolling Stock

49
25-ton brake van, U.K.

50
Continental pattern 20-ton goods van, U.K.

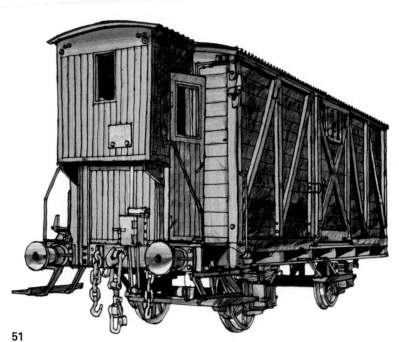

51
20-ton goods van with brakesman's perch, U.K.

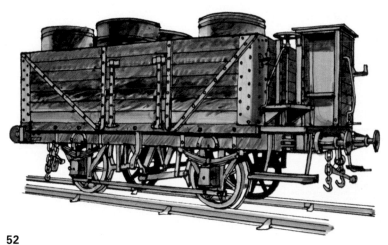

52
12-ton wagon with brakesman's perch, U.K.

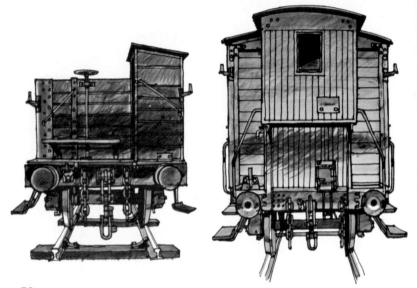

53
End view of the wagon and van, U.K.

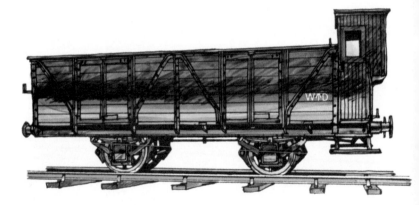

54
10-ton high-sided wagon, U.K.

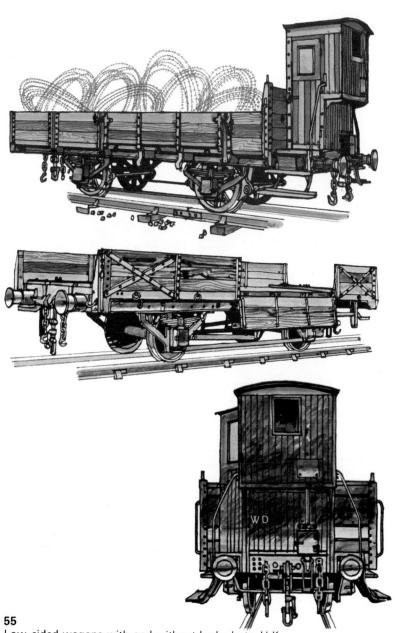

55
Low-sided wagons with and without brake huts, U.K.

56
Baldwin 2-8-0 freight locomotive, U.S.A.

57
Baldwin 4-6-0 mixed traffic locomotive, U.S.A.

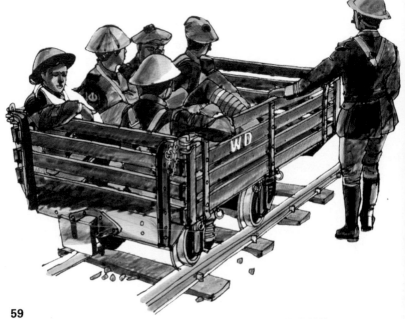

58
Improvised trolley for transporting wounded, U.K.

59
'P' class dual purpose wagon (60 cm gauge) for wounded, U.K.

Monorail and Suspension Devices

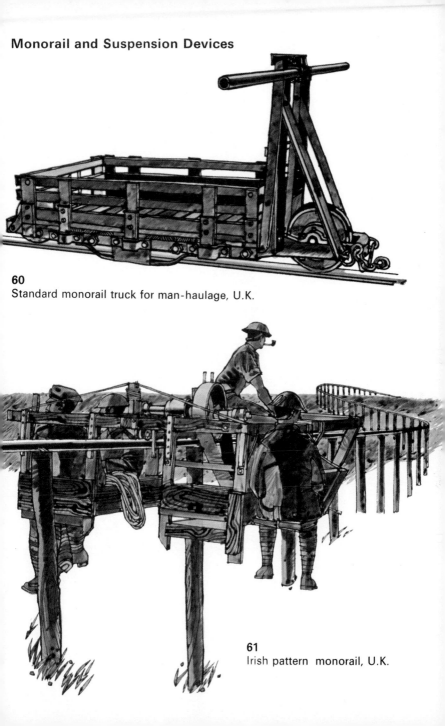

60
Standard monorail truck for man-haulage, U.K.

61
Irish pattern monorail, U.K.

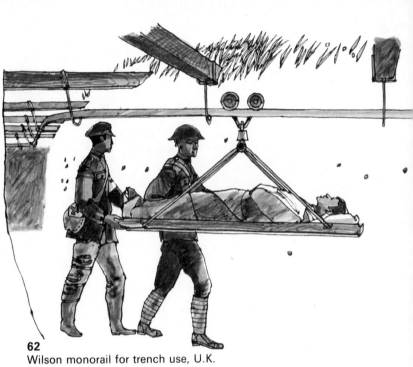

62
Wilson monorail for trench use, U.K.

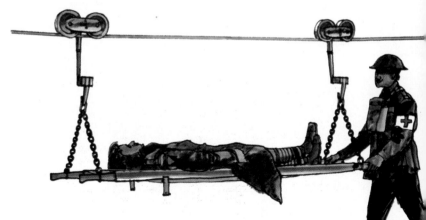

63
Aerial ropeway, U.K.

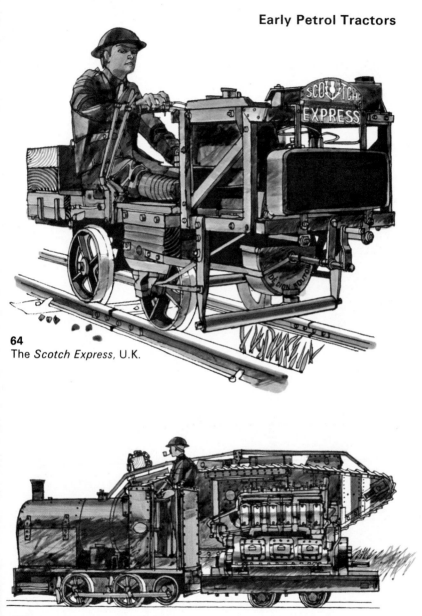

64
The *Scotch Express*, U.K.

65
McEwan Pratt 10 hp tractor shunting, U.K.

66
McEwan Pratt 10 hp tractor with cab, U.K.

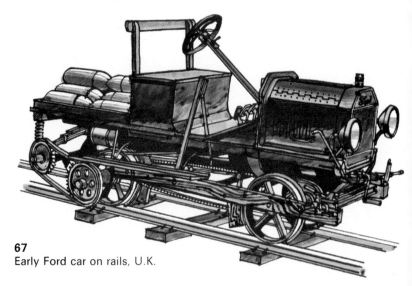

67
Early Ford car on rails, U.K.

68
Crewe tractor in road trim, U.K.

69
Crewe tractor on rail wheels, U.K.

70
Rail motor lorry, Austria

71
Ford rail motor lorry, E. Africa

Pugs (60 cm gauge)
1914-18

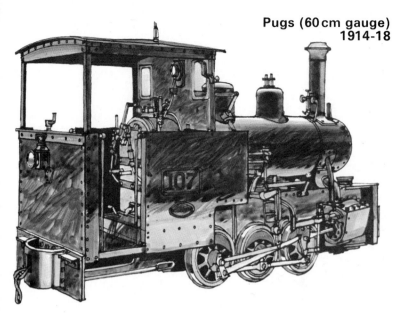

72
Hudson 0-6-0WT, U.K.

73
Barclay 0-6-0WT, U.K.

**Pugs (60 cm gauge)
1914-18**

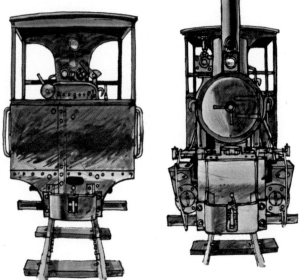

74
Hudson and Barclay comparison, U.K.

75
Baldwin 0-6-0ST, U.S.A. for France

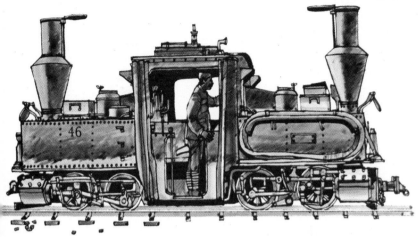

76
Pechot 0-4-4-0T, France

77
Feldbahn 0-8-0T, Germany

Variations on a Theme
(60 cm gauge)

78
Hunslet 4-6-0T U.K.

79
Baldwin 4-6-0T, U.S.A. for U.K.

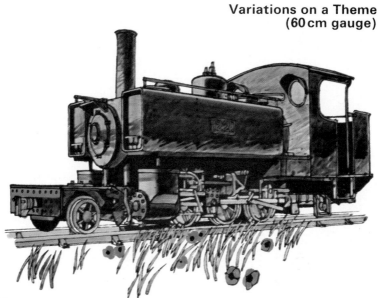

80
ALCO 2-6-2T, U.S.A. for U.K.

81
Baldwin 2-6-2T, U.S.A.

Variations on a Theme
(60 cm gauge)

82
Baldwin 4-6-0T under repair, U.S.A.

83
Hunslet 4-6-0T with condensing gear, U.K.

**Picking up Water
(60 cm gauge)**

84
Taking water via a water lifter, Allied

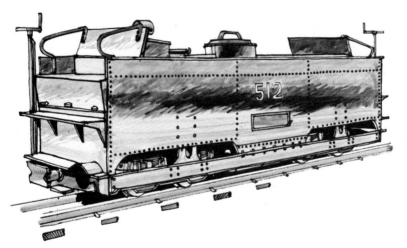

85
Auxiliary water tender, Germany

Too Much Water in the Wrong Place
(60 cm gauge)

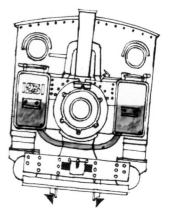
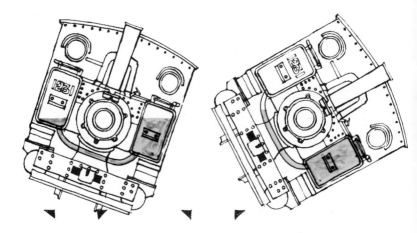

86
Events leading to derailment by water

Too Much Water in the Wrong Place
(60 cm gauge)

87
ALCO 2-6-2T after overbalancing

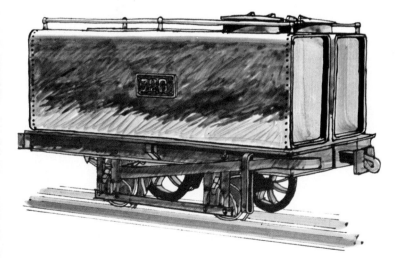

88
Using an improvised tender

Carrying Liquid in Bulk

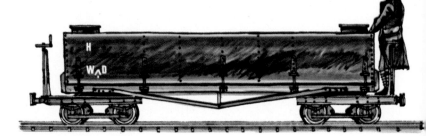

89
'H' class bogie tank wagon, U.K.

91
'G' class 4-wheeled tank wagon, U.K.

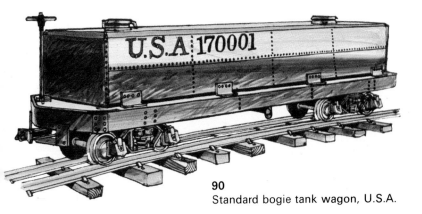

90
Standard bogie tank wagon, U.S.A.

92
Improvised tank wagon, France

93
Deutz 4-wheeled tractor, Germany

94
Baldwin petrol tractor, U.S.A.

Petrol Tractors

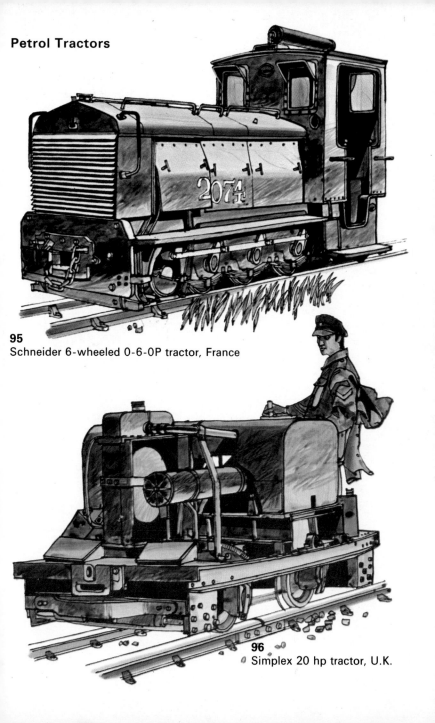

95
Schneider 6-wheeled 0-6-0P tractor, France

96
Simplex 20 hp tractor, U.K.

97
Simplex 40 hp 'open' tractor, U.K.

98
Simplex 40 hp 'protected' tractor, U.K.

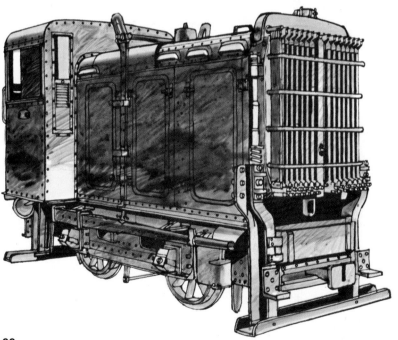

99
British Westinghouse petrol-electric tractor, U.K.

Petrol-Electric Tractors

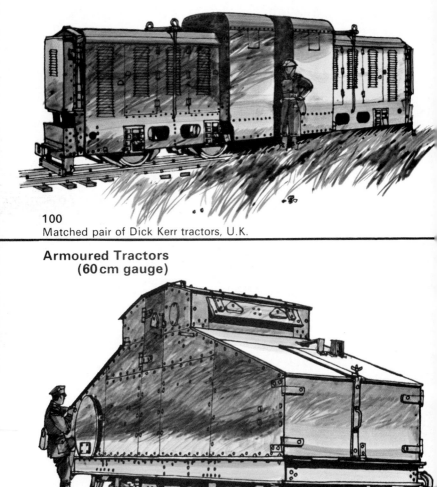

100
Matched pair of Dick Kerr tractors, U.K.

Armoured Tractors
(60 cm gauge)

102
Decauville-Crochat petrol-electric tractor, France

101
A petrol-electric tractor in service, U.K.

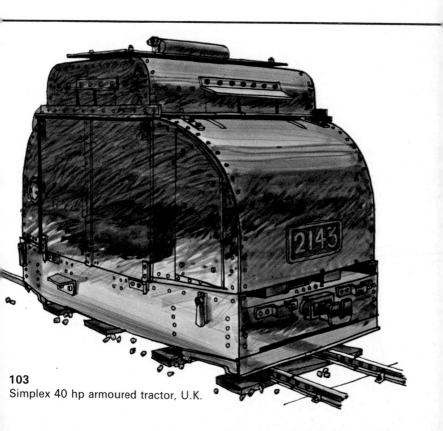

103
Simplex 40 hp armoured tractor, U.K.

Armoured Tractors
(60 cm gauge)

104
Hall-Scott gasoline tractor, U.S.A.

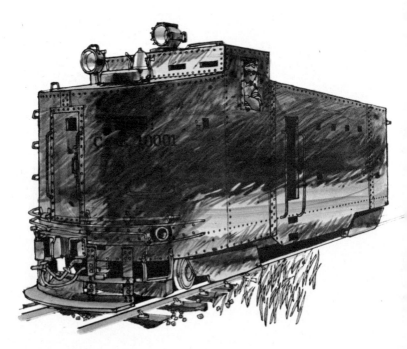

105
Prototype oil-electric locomotive, U.S.A.

106
Drewry 'B' type trolley chassis, U.K.

107
Motor trolley in use for stretcher patients, U.K.

108
Motor trolley ready for running, U.K.

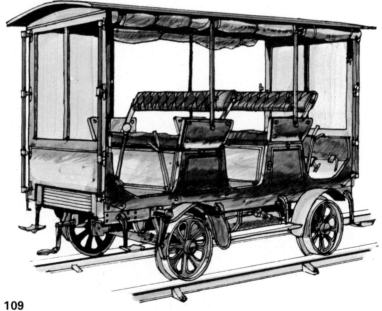

109
Drewry passenger motor trolley, U.K.

Metre Gauge Rolling Stock

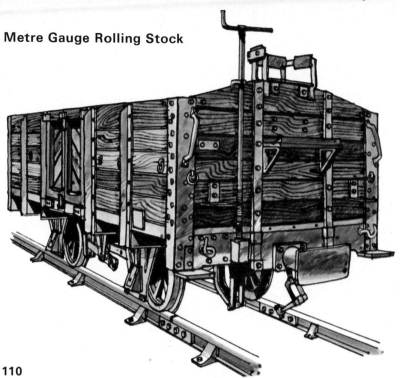

110
Metre gauge 4-wheeled wagon, U.K. for Belgium

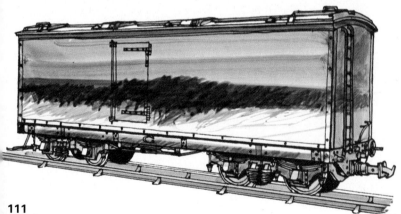

111
Metre gauge refrigerator van

Workshop Trains
(60 cm gauge)

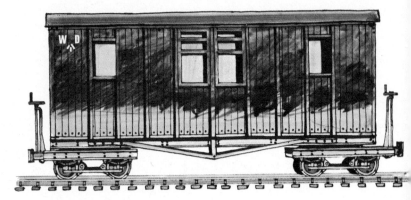

112
Office van for workshop train, U.K.

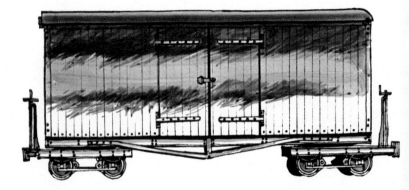

113
Tool and stores wagon, U.K.

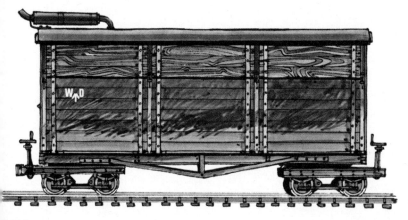

114
Machinery van, closed up U.K.

115
Machinery van operating, U.K.

116
60 cm gauge railway in abandoned village

Light Railway Loads
(60 cm gauge)

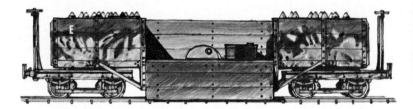

117
'E' class wagon loaded with heavy shells

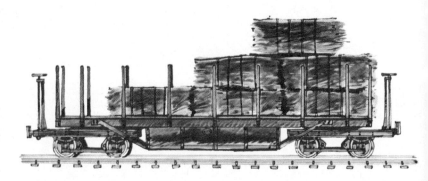

118
'F' class flat well-wagon with forage

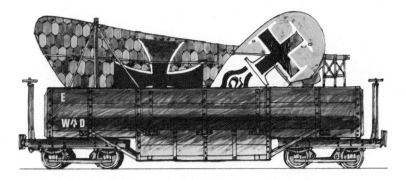

119
'E' class wagon with wreckage (aircraft)

120
'D' class wagon with ballast

Rolling Stock Jigsaws
(60 cm gauge)

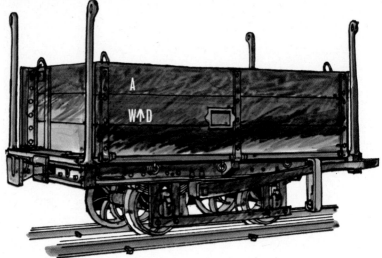

121
'A' class 4-wheeled wagon erected, U.K.

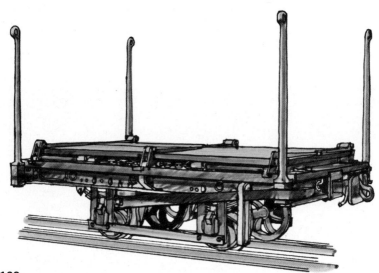

122
'A' class wagon as a flat car, U.K.

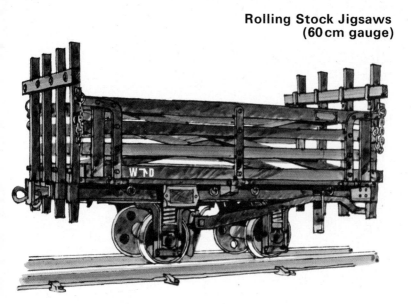

123
'P' class 4-wheeled wagon fully assembled, U.K.

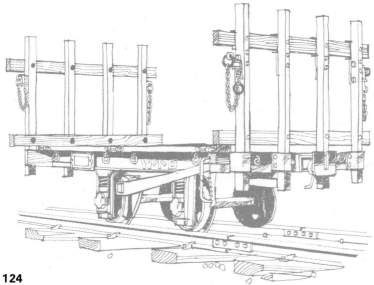

124
'P' class wagon stripped, U.K.

Rolling Stock Jigsaws
(60 cm gauge)

125
'B' class 4-wheeled wagon, U.K.

126
'C' class (double B) bogie wagon, U.K.

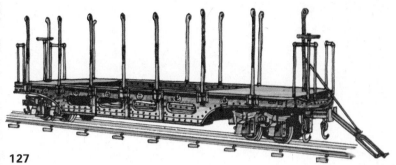

127
Standard well-wagon assembled, France

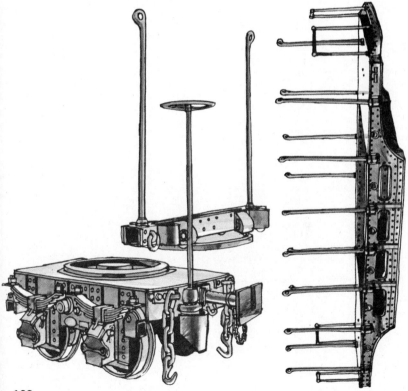

128
Details of French well-wagon components

Rolling Stock Jigsaws (60 cm gauge)

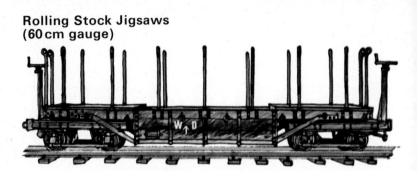

129
'F' class well-wagon side and end, U.K.

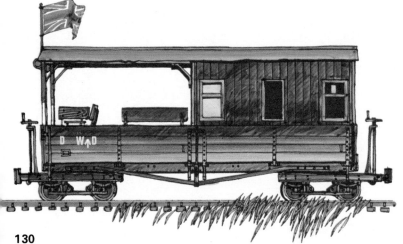

130
V.I.P. coach of British 2nd Army, 1918

131
Office coach, Canadian Corps, 1917

Special Vehicles for 60 cm gauge

132
Metal bodied tip-truck (all armies)

133
American Tip truck, U.S.A.

134
American pattern tip truck, upright and tipped, U.S.A. for U.K.

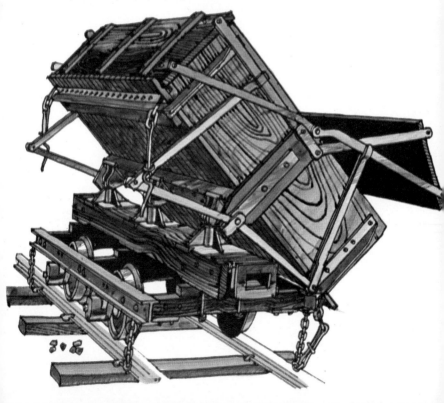

Carrying Howitzers on 60 cm gauge

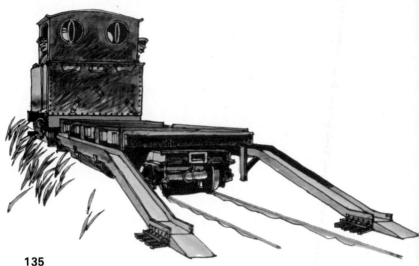

135
Modified bogie well-wagon

136
Loading howitzer via ramps

137
Howitzer on wagon

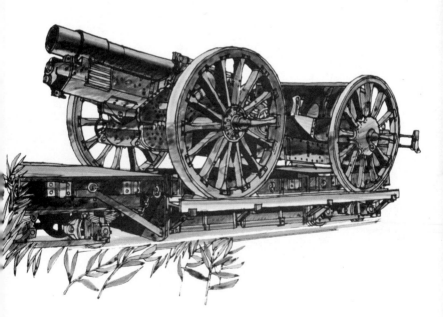

138
Howitzer and limber in travelling position

Transporting Tanks by Rail
(Standard Gauge)

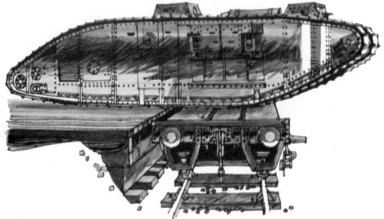

139
Tank approaching Rectank wagon

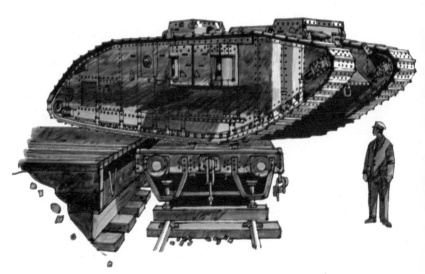

140
Tank pivoting on wagon

141
Tank being secured for transport

142
Rectank wagon with tank in place

Transporting Tanks in the Field

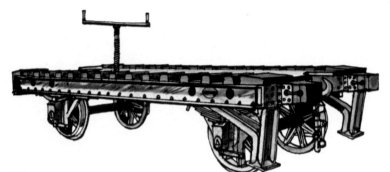

143
Ramp wagon for loading tanks

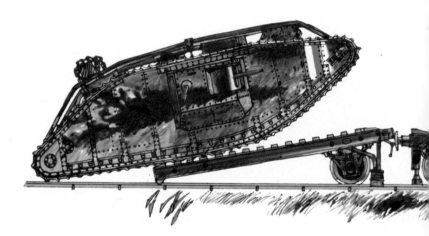

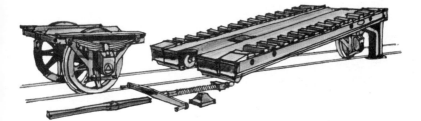

144
Ramp wagon ready for use

145
Loading tanks via a ramp wagon

Transporting Tanks in the Field

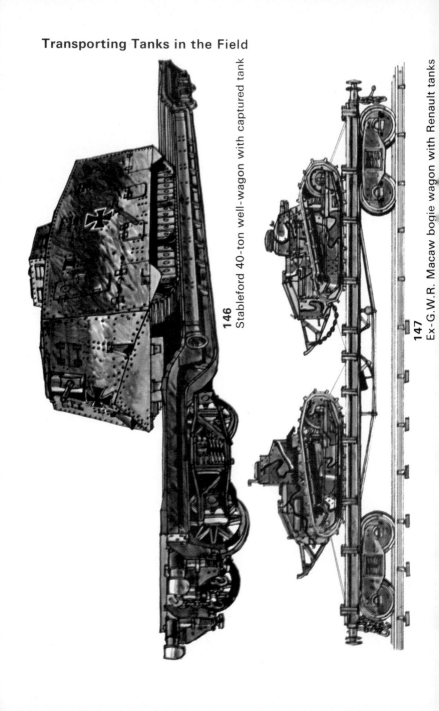

146
Stableford 40-ton well-wagon with captured tank

147
Ex-G.W.R. Macaw bogie wagon with Renault tanks

148
35-ton breakdown crane, U.K.

Standard Gauge Shunting Locomotives

149
Baldwin 2-6-2T U.S.A. for U.K.

150
Baldwin 0-6-0T, U.S.A. for U.K.

151
The 'Blighty' train

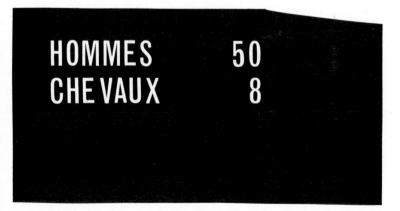

152
50 hommes, 8 chevaux

153
Moving men on the 60 cm gauge

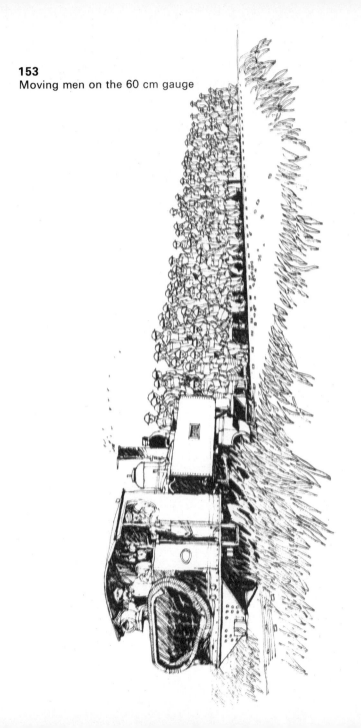

154
Ambulance wagons for the 60 cm gauge

Armoured Train 1918-style

155
Czech armoured trolley for standard gauge

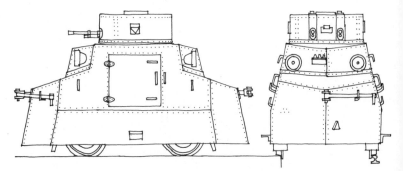

156
Czech trolley – general arrangement

DESCRIPTIVE NOTES

AMERICAN CIVIL WAR (mid-1860s)

The American Civil War, in the mid-1860s, saw the first real use of railways for military purposes. They became important by the accident of geography; distances were so great for the Union armies in particular as they advanced that strong communication links were vital. Many many mistakes were made, and traffic organisation was so primitive that at times it was calculated that more supply trains were waiting in sidings than were on the move. Nevertheless the war saw the first tentative chords of themes that run through all military railway history: supply, destruction of supply, mounting of guns on rails.

1 A Confederate patrol on the line

Notable were the first primitive attempts, particularly by Confederate forces as seen here, to disrupt enemy supply lines. With plenty of room to manoeuvre, it was comparatively easy for small parties of men to come on a deserted section of line—the more so because the need to patrol such stretches had not yet been fully realised. With single track and primitive repair equipment, even the removal of a few rails and the burning of their sleepers was enough to cause serious disruption. The Confederates also became skilled in ripping up lines likely to be of use to an advancing army; their own railways were comparatively little used and indeed many were dismantled to provide iron for armour plate and other fortification uses.

2 The famous 4-4-0 'The General'

Typical of the available locomotive power was that characteristic type the high-wheeled, spark-arrester-stacked 'American' 4-4-0. This is perhaps the most famous of them all, 'The General', here seen in pre-war guise. It gained fame through being stolen by Union raiders and then recaptured after a breathless chase; it finished the war a wreck and was rebuilt. It still survives as a museum piece, far smarter than it ever was in wartime. It was only one of many similar machines not really well suited to heavy military work; perhaps their only advantage was that they burned wood, so fuel was rarely short.

3/4 Heavy mortar on rail truck (Union troops)

First real attempts to put artillery on rails to make it more mobile were the machines typified by this Union mortar or bombard. It was designed to be pushed in front of a locomotive to a point from which it could shell enemy forces and displays most of the features later common to heavy rail artillery—the crew shield often improvised from available materials, the limited traverse, the need for a massive underframe. This example was built for the Federal forces in Petersburg, Virginia, and is an obvious improvisation with its 'armour' made up mainly from baulks of timber. Like others, it saw little if any effective service. Rail artillery had to wait for a later war to become really useful.

5 Destruction of communications. A Prussian troop train blown up when crossing a bridge at Mezières.

The next serious use of railways came about during the rapid and decisive Franco-Prussian War of 1870, which highlighted many lessons that badly needed learning. The Prussian Army, while not entirely prepared, did have an embryo railway operating organisation and several sections of railway troops (Eisenbahntruppen). These were trained railwaymen (engineers, signalmen, etc.) and trained soldiers, carrying rifles as well as their railway tools. The Prussian railways themselves were efficiently organised to move troops and equipment and their engineers were able to lay strictly military railways, which they did on several occasions. But they had not realised the serious shortage of rolling-stock that would be caused when operating extended lines of communication if an enemy had managed to withdraw in good order; their use of French railways for supply was seriously hampered by this. Nor had the Prussians a really efficient organisation for repairing extensive damage caused by a retreating enemy.

The French, on the other hand, while they had a railway system basically capable of meeting their military requirements, had virtually no military organisation for operating it efficiently. As a result there was total chaos, whole units becoming 'lost' while stores piled up in huge bottlenecks at the receiving stations of Metz and Strasbourg. There was little or no co-operation between the military and the railway authorities and the blame must fall almost entirely on the military.

At the same time, even without an organisation, the French did show what could be done to deny use of railways to an advancing foe. The destruction of bridges, tunnels and trackwork was far vaster than in the American War and, although more might have been done with better organisation—lack of orders saved a number of structures—the Prussians were still greatly impeded. Several Prussian troop and supply trains were even blown up by 'Franc-Tireurs' (irregulars) along with the track or bridge they were traversing. The plate shows a double-headed train which came to grief in this way. The importance of vital junctions was also realised, considerable fighting taking place on the railway for their possession.

The war ended badly for France, but its transport lessons were learnt by both parties. The German empire, as Prussians and her allies became, pressed on with the organisation of an efficient military railway department and the provision of equipment. The French started to put their house in order on the Prussian pattern, creating organisational links between the military and civil authorities, and building strategic railways to fill gaps in their system. The British took an interested note of all the goings-on; they even read learned papers to the Corps of Royal Engineers on the lessons to be learnt. It was certainly the mistakes of this war that laid the basis for sound military use of civilian railways in future major wars; but the next developments were overseas, in the colonies being set up by the major European powers.

COLONIAL LINES: GERMAN SOUTH-WEST AFRICA, 1897-1910

In the last decades of the 19th century and the first one of the 20th century, all the great European powers were constantly expanding their colonial territories, particularly in Africa. Needless to say, the natives usually resented being forcibly civilised and there were constant skirmishes, between them and the settlers, occasionally developing into full scale wars. The Germans were fairly late in the field but, once they started, they did the job of colonisation with their usual thoroughness. South-West Africa, where they were constantly battling with both the climate and the main resident tribe, the Hereros, provides an excellent example of the use of railways in small colonial wars. Starting in 1897, from an open roadstead at Swakopmund where only light equipment could be discharged, the German military authorities constructed a 60-cm. gauge 'field railway' (Feldbahn) inland over the desert of Windhoek, some 382 km. in all. This was regarded as a military railway, was built and operated by an army Railway Brigade (in fact a weak battalion) and, besides supplying the troops and colonists, acted as a proving ground for military light railway equipment.

6 Zwillinge 0-6-0Ts and auxiliary tender (Germany)

Initial motive power of the railway was standard military equipment sent out from army stores. It comprised an unknown number of twin unit 0-6-0Ts known as 'Zwillinge' (twins). These were each composed of two 0-6-0T locomotives permanently coupled back to back and designed, so it was said, to be worked in multiple. In fact, this 'design' extended only to the provision of overlapping footplates and cab roofs of different heights, since the only mechanical connection was the drawbar and, later, a water hose. Each double-unit had a single running number, the individual locomotives having a B (low cab) or A (high cab) suffix. A double unit weighed 14 tons 1·5 cwt in working order, with a wheel diameter of 1 ft 10⅝ in. and a total wheelbase of 17 ft 3½ in.

These units and similar, though slightly stronger, ones delivered later were used both as delivered and, split, as single units ('Illinge'). Because of the long distance between usable water supplies they were soon equipped with auxiliary bogie water tenders, another standard piece of military equipment which even had seats installed for armed escorts. These must have seriously reduced the already small loads that the Zwillinge could haul and they were, in fact, found to be almost useless on steep grades, especially the climb through River Khan Gorge.

7 Krauss 0-8-0T for State Northern Railway

As a result of the weakness of the Zwillinge, two 0-8-0Ts, again to an army design, were ordered from Krauss & Co. in 1901 and sent out to act as bankers on the Khan Gorge section. In practice it appears that they usually took over the train entirely, working in tandem; they could pull 25 tonnes up the severe grades by this method. These locomotives and their successors can be considered as experimental prototypes for the later World War One's 0-8-0Ts. With a boiler pressure of 170 lb/sq in., two outside cylinders $9\frac{7}{16}$ in. by $11\frac{13}{16}$ in., a coupled wheel diameter of $25\frac{5}{8}$ in. and a coupled wheelbase of 16 ft $3\frac{7}{8}$ in., they were rated at 60 h.p. as against the 40 h.p. of an Illing. They also had to tow water trailers.

8 Jung 0-8-0T for State Northern Railway

The 0-8-0Ts were so successful that eighteen similar machines, differing slightly in power and detail design, were produced over the next four years by various makers; no doubt the military were evaluating various items of equipment, notably the Klien-Lindner method of wheelbase articulation, since this locomotive No. 116 (Arnold Jung 814 of 1905) appears to have the jointed coupling rods associated with such a design. It also shows the typical German spark-arrester chimney fitted to most of the locomotives on the State Northern line.

9 Klien-Lindner method of axle articulation

The vital requirement for military 60-cm. gauge railway locomotives was that they should be capable of traversing sharp curves, and that they should not seriously distort light track while doing so. The efforts to solve this problem were essentially similar and probably stemmed from the experiments on 15 in. gauge equipment carried out by the British baronet Sir Arthur Heywood during the 1880s and 1890s. All required linked sleeve axles pivoting to give some side play to the end coupled wheels and

the Klien-Lindner arrangement (sometimes known as the Krauss-Lindner) was the standard German army adaptation for 0-8-0Ts. As can be seen, the two inner axles were fixed normally in the frames. Each outer axle unit comprised a fixed beam axle, in the centre of which was a spherical portion holding a vertical pivot. An outer sleeve being of greater diameter than the main axle, and having the wheels integral with it, was pivoted by this means and could therefore swivel to a limited degree. The coupling rods had a form of universal joint to give some flexibility and the swivelling axles were linked by yokes to ensure accurate and symmetrical 'tracking'.

9a Feldbahn 0-8-0T and auxiliary tender

The end result of the Swakopmund experiments was the 'standard' German army 60-cm. gauge 0-8-0T, equipped with spark-arrester, Klien-Lindner radial axles and an enlarged version of the old auxiliary tender. It is fully described in Plate 77, and the tender in Plate 85, but is shown here to illustrate the logical conclusion of the South-West African equipment programme.

10 Motor inspection trolley (60 cm. gauge)

The German colonial military railways were among the first to realise the value of internal combustion engined equipment for use on light field railways. Typical of the early vehicles is this 4-wheeled petrol-engined machine used on the Swakopmund-Windhoek line during the early years of the present century for inspection purposes. Not much is known about it but it does show the typical arrangement of reversible box-seats with the engine stowed underneath them, a feature common to most inspection trolleys for the next thirty years and more. Typical, too, is the haughty mien of the officer passenger and the humble attitude of his 'other-rank' chauffeur.

11 **Drewry inspection car and trailer** (U.K.)

Just to make the point that engined trolley design appears to have progressed only slowly is this drawing of a 'standard' Drewry Car Co. trolley for 4 ft 8½ in. gauge, with a No. 2 matching trailer. This car was in use in the 1930s and is of very much the same basic design as its earlier German colleague.

MILITARY RAILWAY OPERATING PROBLEMS: SOUTH AFRICAN WAR, 1899-1902

Although railways had previously been used for supply and troop transport in various campaigns and specific military lines had been constructed especially in the Soudan, the first extensive *purely military* use of railways in war came during the South African 'Boer' War of 1899-1902. This campaign, owing to the vast arid distances to be covered by both sides, saw the rapid development of all facets of such operation; use of civilian railways to transport military troops and equipment; bringing of civilian railways under military operational control; wholesale destruction of railways by a retreating army and their consequent reconstruction and operation as purely

military lines; guerilla warfare against vulnerable lines of communication; and the development of military transport techniques in general. It saw also the first effective use of armoured trains and of heavy rail-borne artillery. Indeed the British used it, as they did for other arms, as a valuable training ground for military engineers and a proving ground for new techniques.

Certainly the war gave much scope for developments both in operating and in maintaining railways under war conditions. A feature of the campaign was the easy way in which mounted Boer 'commandos' were able to infiltrate British-held territory and blow up portions of line to disrupt traffic. The engineers became adept at repairing such breaches—one of their boasts was that a normal 'break' discovered at dawn would be repaired in general before 9.00 a.m. Much more serious was the widespread destruction caused by the Boers when retreating over their own territory.

In particular bridges and other engineering works were thoroughly destroyed. This severely hampered the cumbrous British Army which depended on its rail communications and drastic measures were taken to restore the lines to traffic. The plate shows a typical improvisation carried out on the 3 ft 6 in. gauge line from Elandsfontein to Koomati Poort in the Boer Transvaal during the British advance in 1900.

12 **Restoring rail communications**

Some idea of the destruction caused can be gained from the fact that it took reconstruction parties two months to cover the 140 miles or so between 'railhead' and this point at Kaapmuiden where the line crossed the Kaap river. This was the last major bridge on the line and a fairly common expedient was resorted to: the bridge had been so seriously damaged that a deviation and low-level temporary structure were decided on, the work being completed within six days. As can be seen, the deviation which was composed of trestles and 'crib' piers was very sharply curved and with maximum gradients of no less than 1 in 18·5. The level of flooding in the river—which was subject to flash floods at short notice—had been calculated at 20 ft, so rail level was set at $21\frac{1}{2}$ ft above water. The illustration also shows the hazards of using such quick expedients to restore traffic—the wreckage of one train that came to grief on it can clearly be seen.

13 No. 18 armoured train and its operating area

Another 'first' for the British in the South African War was the widespread use of armoured trains both to patrol and protect their lines of communication and to harass Boer commandos actively. Early experiments in Cape Colony were not very effective since the trains were very weak and armed only with rifles and Maxim machine guns. Thus a determined enemy force with light artillery could effectively neutralise them and the trains achieved a bad reputation; indeed most people probably think of them in terms of the one in which Mr (later Sir) Winston Churchill was ignominiously captured by the Boers.

Yet this gives a very unfair picture of the work of armoured trains as a whole. Their weakness was recognised, success-

ful experiments were made with quick firing naval guns and, towards the end of 1900, a proper controlling organisation was set up for them. From that time on, armoured trains played a steadily increasing part in the railway war and by 1902 there were no less than 20. The later pattern armoured train, shown in Plate 13, was a formidable weapon and several times fought successful duels with complete Boer commandos caught in the act of crossing the railway. On the most famous occasion, the Boer commander De Wet was cut off from his wagons by no less than four trains which at the cost of only two wounded men were able to capture all his ammunition and explosives.

More commonly gun-armed trains were used to patrol weakly held stretches of line and to drive Boers away from portions of line that had been blown up, in this way it was possible quickly to repair breaks and some trains even carried repair material with them.

They were also adept at coming to the rescue of beleaguered stations, rather in the manner of the U.S. 7th Cavalry, the attackers usually retiring soon after the armoured monster loomed over the horizon. The late pattern train, then, was an effective fighting unit. It normally consisted of a locomotive in the middle, pulling or pushing armoured vans containing living accommodation, searchlight generators and telegraph instruments. At the opposite side of the locomotive was a water tank truck and next to this an armoured wagon mounting a 3, 6 or more often 12-pounder quick-firing gun. At each end of the train were armoured trucks each containing two Maxim guns and an infantry section armed with rifles. The train often pushed in front of it a loaded bogie wagon fitted with strong cow-catchers; this was used both to sweep obstructions off the line and to explode contact mines, in a number of cases saving the train itself from damage.

14 Bogie Maxim gun truck, standard pattern

Basic armament of all armoured trains from beginning to end of the war were the armoured machine gun trucks. These were bogie vehicles carrying either two Maxim machine guns—successors to the not entirely successful Gatling—or one of the light 1-pounder Nordenfeldt cannon, or a mixture of these weapons. The 1-pounder was a quick-firing weapon very easy to transport and much loved by the Boers for its rapid rate of fire. They used it even more extensively than the British who dubbed it the 'pom-pom' because of its characteristic noise when firing rapidly.

The most widely used pattern of Maxim truck was based on a standard, roofed bogie wagon and carried two Maxims plus a section of infantry armed with rifles. The sides and one end were armoured with $\frac{1}{2}$-in. steel plate, leaving only a narrow gap under the roof to admit light and air; they were pierced at intervals with horizontal loopholes to allow kneeling fire. These slits were staggered on each side and fitted with sliding covers. Near the inner end of each vehicle there was a masked port each side for a Maxim and at the outer end a fighting compartment cut off from the main compartment by overlapping steel screens. This end compartment was armoured only to waist level and contained a shielded Maxim capable of firing

down the line or to either side. Its upper part was also armoured to protect a searchlight operator who sat above the maxim and whose head and shoulders projected into a small 'turret' behind the roof-mounted searchlight. The leading Maxim van usually carried the train's commanding officer, and contained a telephone linked to the other vehicles, and a vacuum brake control valve.

15 Protected bogie truck for supply trains

This was designed specifically for use in flat country and could be quickly constructed locally. It consisted of a standard bogie truck, armoured with lengths of rail in clips at each side to a height of 5 ft, one rail being omitted to provide a continuous firing slit. The ends of the truck were protected by walls of sleepers on which a Maxim could be mounted and had a canvas-awning roof to keep the sun off—hence its use only in flat country where plunging fire would not be encountered. The great advantages of the vehicle were that it could be quickly constructed to meet an emergency and that its armouring could be used to repair a break in the line if the need arose! This type of truck was extensively used both on armoured trains and as escort trucks for supply trains.

16 Early pattern 1-pounder gun truck

With the exception of Maxim trucks and the large gun wagons, most armoured train vehicles were 4-wheelers. This is an early pattern gun truck accommodating a 1-pounder pom-pom and consisting simply of a goods wagon with additional side plating and a sun-awning. Most of the early trains were named and this belonged to train No. 3 'Cock o' the North'.

17/18 Early pattern 12-pounder gun trucks

Early experiments with armoured trains had shown that they needed some weapon heavier than the Maxims and 1-pounder pom-poms to fight off Boer attacks. In addition it was desirable for them to be able to act offensively when needed. From about 1900 on, therefore, all trains included at least one gun truck normally coupled ahead of the engine and mounting one or more quick-firing guns of naval pattern. Most common to start with were the light 3-pounders but by 1902 many trains were fitted with the very effective 12-pounder Q.F. rifled gun.

Plate 17 shows layout and variations on the early pattern of 12-pounder gun truck as used by various armoured trains. These were made up of steel plating fixed on a standard bogie wagon and provided with a shrapnel-proof roof against plunging fire. The two earliest (Plate 18) were partially open above the waist, some parts having steel sheeting pierced for loopholes. They each mounted two guns but, possibly as a relic of their naval origin these were mounted ship-fashion as 'casemate' weapons, that is to say they were each to one side of the vehicle and able, because of this positioning, to fire through an arc on that side only. Each gun was pedestal-mounted, and provided with a sheet-steel crew shield fabricated in railway workshops which was intended to protect the gun layer and loader from direct fire.

19 Late pattern 12-pounder gun truck

The disadvantages of the early pattern truck were realised as the war progressed, and later trains had a much more effective design, 13 in all being built. This was again based on a standard bogie wagon underframe suitably strengthened but carried only one gun on a central pedestal or 'turret' with an all-round field of fire. To allow this the central portion of the wagon sides was built out in semi-circular sponsons. The crew was protected from direct fire by an all-enclosing horseshoe-shaped steel shield with rear flaps, and from plunging fire by deflector plates. The wagons were built up with massive sleeper and iron sides and roofs over each end to provide blast-proof ammunition magazines; these sides also gave shelter to the spare crew members and were sloped downward towards each end to allow the gun to fire along the track at maximum depression. The vehicle could be fitted with a folding awning for protection against the sun. This was supported at each end by a pole on the centre line of the wagon and, when in position, it naturally interfered with firing. It was therefore designed to be collapsed quickly to one side if required.

The Boer War also saw the first serious attempts at using heavy artillery on railway trucks; the idea was to reproduce in inland areas the effect achieved in coastal regions by naval bombardment, and to provide quick and heavy support for our forces. Two patterns of weapon were tried out, the 6-in. gun and the 9·2-in. gun, both of naval origin.

20 9·2-in. naval gun on experimental rail mounting

This, the forerunner of future rail-borne artillery, was the heaviest weapon mounted on railway wagons up to that date—and considering that the South African gauge was only 3 ft 6 in., it was a very fine effort.

The gun was mounted fore and aft, with only very limited traverse, on a vehicle made up partly from the frame of an old locomotive, and to bring it into action it was necessary to lower heavy screw jacks at each side. The wagon was provided with a built-in ammunition hoist for lifting the heavy shells into the gun breech. This gun was fired only experimentally but apparently with complete success.

21 6-in. naval gun firing from a railway mounting

Two 6-in. naval guns were however put into service and used quite extensively. They were installed on pedestal mountings fixed to strengthened bogie wagons and initially were fired fore-and-aft, or with limited traverse from specially laid, curved sidings. In this form they took part in the engagements at Modder River and Fourteen Streams. Later, one was converted as shown for attachment to No. 2 armoured train and was frequently employed either with the train or as a surprise addition to the armament of a fortified station likely to come under attack; in the latter case it was brought up under cover of darkness and left there. The modifications consisted of two pivoted girders at each side which could be quickly swung out to act as stabilisers and allow the gun a 360° field of fire.

The engineers claimed that the gun could be brought into action inside five minutes and it was in frequent use up to the end of the war without damaging its mounting or wagon.

EXPERIMENTS IN THE EARLY 20th CENTURY

All army railway departments after the experiences of the British in South Africa recognised two major problems: military railways often needed to be laid quickly, over unprepared ground; and they needed to be as inconspicuous as possible to avoid unwelcome attention from an enemy. Almost simultaneously in Germany and Britain, men invented a gyroscopically balanced monorail and offered it to the military.

22 Brennan monorail car (U.K.)

First to demonstrate a workable vehicle —approximately two hours in front of his rival—was Mr Louis Brennan, C.B., who produced the vehicle shown and demonstrated it at Gillingham on 10 November 1909. It was a petrol/electric machine using an 80 h.p. Wolseley engine driving two Siemens motors via a dynamo, and with a separate generator set for powering its two 'gyrostats'. It initially impressed both civil and military reporters by its steadiness and the ease with which track was laid but nothing came of it. In retrospect the basic problems of power and the difficulty of providing detachable trailers as opposed to fixed 'trains' seem to have outweighed the advantages.

23 Scheil gyro-car (Germany)

The same can undoubtedly be said for Brennan's competitor, Herr Scheil, who demonstrated his much smaller vehicle in the Berlin Zoo. At a mere 17 ft in length and with a capacity of only half-a-dozen people it was dismissed by the British press as 'a mere toy'; it disappeared into limbo like its competitor.

24 Wolseley-engined petrol tractor (U.K.)

More promising, eventually, than the various monorail experiments that took place between the wars, was the early development of petrol-engined tractors. Little is known in detail about this rather curious little Wolseley-engined machine but it was produced to War Office order and was apparently narrow gauge—almost certainly 1 ft 6 in. or 2 ft 6 in. gauge. The War Office was responsible for a number of experimental internal-combustion-engined machines at this period and, indeed, used them on various depot lines besides stockpiling some 2 ft 6 in. gauge versions in its Royal Engineers siege park.

WORLD WAR ONE: EARLY DAYS OF RAILWAY OPERATION 1914

25 Belgian locomotive on canal bridge as rebuilt by Royal Engineers

Of the major powers engaged at the outbreak of World War One only Britain and Russia had no master plan for use of railway transport. The German mobilisation and plan of offensive depended on it, the French had a scheme for bringing their main-line railways under military control, the Austrians had a big military railway department. As the aggressors, Germany and Austria could utilise their railways fully, and the Allies on the Western Front in particular found that the speed of the German advance had largely disrupted what plans there were. The French railways, although under military control, had lost a considerable amount of stock and many important engineering works near the front lines were destroyed before the fronts stabilised. For the first two years of war in fact the position can fairly be symbolised by this picture: rapid improvisation. This elderly Belgian 0-8-0 of unknown parentage, saved during the long retreat, is typical of the motley collection of locomotives scraped up to cope with the supply requirements of not only the French but also the British armies. The improvised but sturdy reconstruction of the canal bridge epitomises the lessons learnt by the British Royal Engineers during the South African War. Yet it was still improvisation; it was not until 1916 that locomotives and rolling stock requisitioned from British main line railways came to supplement the hard pressed French machines, and it was nearly a year later when standard locomotives and rolling-stock appeared in quantity.

26 Badges of the French military railways

All railway lines in France, both standard and metre gauge were immediately affected by World War One. Most intimately involved, of course, were those in the battle zones and rear areas which were put under direct military control (Le Direction de l'Arrière—Rear Area Control). The railway transport side in particular was then formed into the Service des Chemins de Fer (S.C.F.) designed to ensure best use of all railway tracks and material. The Military Railway Engineers operated mainly in the front line, responsibility for most of the system being entrusted to the civilian staff called up into so-called 'Sections de Chemins de Fer de Campagne'. Each section operated in principle between 100 and 200 km. of line. For various reasons many of these personnel still used their civilian clothing at least initially, and various identifying badges were used.

The standard identification was a symbolised 2-2-2 locomotive cut out in outline on cloth and worn on the right arm. It was originally in red on a blue-black coat and later, when the horizon-blue was in general use, the badge was changed to a dark blue. The other main means of identification was a brassard or armband worn on the upper left arm to denote the function of its wearer. The one shown is for a member of the railways' 'home guard', the 'garde-voies et communications', consisting of armed railwaymen who protected vital points on the system.

Cross-Channel Transport

Alone of the European participants in World War One, the United Kingdom had the problem of having first to ship all its men and equipment across the Channel before they could join in the fighting. For the first two years—when the war was always expected to end with the next offensive—this opera-

tion was carried out fairly laboriously using conventional cargo steamers and the existing port facilities. By the end of 1916, however, it was realised that something more elaborate was needed and a complete new port was gradually built up on a plot of land at Richborough just north of Sandwich on the Kent coast.

Originally a small barge depot, by the end of 1917 it had expanded to 2200 acres of sidings, berths and workshops. It was a training base, a boatyard and a ferry terminal, being served by some 60 miles of sidings. These were connected to the South Eastern & Chatham Railway and shunted day and night by a motley fleet of small tank locomotives such as that shown in Plate 27. It was also the main British terminal for a major train ferry service to Dunkirk and Calais from February, 1918, onwards, two ships being specially built. There was a plan to develop the port commercially after the war but it came to nothing and the whole complex slowly rotted away.

Much war material, including many items of railway equipment was shipped over to France in seagoing barges. These eventually reached sizes of about 1000 tons capacity and to accommodate them a major rerouting of the River Stour was undertaken. A complete horseshoe bend was drained and filled, a channel being dug across its base and a long wharf built thereon capable of handling ten barges; it was later extended to hold twenty-four.

27 Shunting locomotives at Richborough

The sidings were shunted by a motley collection of small steam locomotives acquired from various civilian sources. Most were typical industrial 'pugs' exemplified by this 0-4-0ST built by Andrew Barclay Ltd. at Kilmarnock. Positive identification of this particular locomotive is uncertain but a typical machine of the type had 14 in. by 21 in. cylinders, a boiler pressure of 160 lb/sq. in., wheelbase of 5 ft 6 in. and a coupled wheel diameter of 3 ft.

28 Arrangements for docking train ferry

Train ferries were something new for the Army and considerable doubt was expressed as to whether they would be successful on a cross-Channel run. The advantages to be gained were so great, however, that orders were placed for three ships (one for another service) and a special stern-loading dock was commissioned. This was a hinged iron 'bridge', pivoted at the shore end and raised or lowered by means of counterweights working within a gantry at the seaward end. By this means the rail level at the junction with the ship could be adjusted by up to 5 ft on either side of the horizontal—quite enough since the variation in tidal levels is very small at Richborough. Additionally the bridge could be tilted to allow for up to a 5° list in the ship. The latter was warped into exact alignment by being laid alongside a wooden jetty and moved stern first until it snugged into curved piers exactly fitting the ship's stern contours. The bridge could then be lowered until positive location was made on the stern and the tracks were then automatically linked through from shore to ship. Tracks were at 11 ft 6 in. centres and to continental loading gauge.

29 The cross-Channel train ferry: layout of ship

As can be seen, the ferry steamers were shallow draught vessels with a single train deck carrying four tracks; they could be loaded via the stern only and had both stern and bow ballast tanks to enable rail level above water to be adjusted within reasonable limits for easy matching with the shore. Each was 363 ft 6 in. long, having a mean draught (loaded) of 9 ft 6 in., a displacement of some 3654 tons and a cargo capacity of 850 tons; track space was provided for 54 loaded 4-wheel 10-ton wagons or their equivalent. Under reasonable weather conditions they could achieve 12 knots.

30/31 Ferry Steamer; bow and stern views

These views show the very wide beam of these shallow draught vessels, a total of 61 ft 6 in. or nearly a sixth of the ship's length. As can be seen, the train deck was largely open except directly underneath the boat deck, and a catwalk was provided round the bulwarks except at the extreme stern. With their ease of loading and unloading, and the advantages of not having to dismantle their cargo, these vessels performed invaluable service; it was said that they were the equivalent of at least six 8000 ton conventional cargoships.

R.O.D. CONTRASTS (U.K.)

32 Standard 2-8-0 goods locomotive

As the war progressed into 1917, the motley collection of R.O.D. locomotives was greatly supplemented, though never entirely replaced by, a number of standard designs. Foremost among these was the British designed and built 2-8-0 goods locomotive shown in this plate. It would appear that when the need for a standard heavy locomotive became apparent, the War Department first investigated existing British designs to see if any were suitable for purchase 'off the shelf'. Their choice fell on the heavy 2-8-0 freight locomotive designed by J. G. Robinson for the Great Central Railway. The class had been in service since 1911 and proved both robust and reliable; it was taken into service with few modifications except for the addition of steam heating gear and the Westinghouse air brake, 521 examples in all being produced to military order by various British manufacturers. Leading dimensions were: boiler pressure; 180 lb/psi cylinders 21 in. by 26 in., coupled wheel dia. 4 ft 8 in.

33 Requisitioned goods locomotive pulling a heavy gun

The use of railborne artillery was tentatively explored during the American Civil War; it became a reality for medium sized guns during the South African Wars at the end of the 19th century; it came into full flower during World War One with the development of monster long-range guns that could effectively be fired only from battleships, static coast defence works . . . or from railway wagons. Such guns of 11- or 12-in. calibre, and even in one or two cases up to 15 or 16 in., were far too massive to be towed around the roads but did have a definite value in long range harassment of an enemy's communications and rear areas. The de-

moralising effect of heavy shells falling regularly on a village or town was considerable. At the same time the guns could not always be dug into a static position since they were vulnerable to a sudden advance and if located could often be shelled or bombed. Both sides, on the Western Front in particular, therefore, produced a number of special carrying wagons such as that shown here. They were normally built up from heavy steel box frames forming a braced girder in which the gun was installed, and mounted on multi-wheel bogies to keep down the axleload. The gun had a firing and maintenance crew of anything up to thirty men and a typical one could fire at a rate of some 4 to 6 shells an hour. Each gun normally had its own locomotive, usually an impressed civilian goods engine, and one or more service vehicles. Guns were moved from position to position as required and were frequently sited so that they could either be hidden in tunnels from which they emerged to fire, or established in a cutting which gave some protection. One problem was that the weight of the weapon gave it only a very limited traverse without overbalancing so that either a line had to be found pointing in the required direction or a special siding had to be laid. This was often laid on a constant curve, a so-called 'firing curve', that enabled direction to be varied by shunting the gun truck from one point to another along the line.

RAIL-BORNE ARTILLERY AGAIN

34 Methods of siting heavy railborne artillery (France)

With the static nature of World War One all the belligerents found some use for super-heavy artillery to shell the enemy rear areas. The French in particular found themselves embarrassingly short of purpose-built weapons and had initially to round up a motley collection of naval and coast defence barrels (so far as super-heavy artillery was concerned, the important part was the gun barrel with its associated breech and recoil mechanism. The mounting could be fabricated to suit the task in hand). The problems of mounting these guns on mobile platforms were twofold. For calibres above about 155 mm. (c. 5·5 in.), the gun could only be fired at a comparatively small angle to the railway track unless supported by elaborate sponsons; and the recoil of such huge pieces was very difficult to absorb without damage to the track. This last problem was often worsened by the need to fire howitzers especially at near-maximum elevation. The motley nature of the early French artillery-on-rails (A.L.V.F.—*artillerie lourde sur vioe ferrée*) enables us to illustrate several of the ways of installing such weapons for firing.

(a) 400-mm. calibre howitzer, ex-French navy, was mounted on a high, revolving platform, since it was normally fired at maximum elevation and thus most of the recoil shock was downwards. Its stability was assured by what amounted to spring jacks bearing down on transverse beams and anchored amidships to a shallow pit. The vehicle was self-contained and had a semi-automatic loading mechanism allowing it to fire a shell every three minutes or so.

(b) 240-mm. gun, 1884 model. This, mounted on a massive chassis, required a special pit to accept the elevation and was a coastal defence gun mounted on rigid trunnions. Its recoil was countered by what was termed the 'glissement' or slippage method, the shock being transmitted to the chassis which in turn recoiled several feet along the track. It was restrained by inclined springs and was winched back into position manually while being reloaded.

(c) This 285-mm. weapon was also rigidly mounted, using massive platform blocks to support the weight of the weapon but did not require special pits. It took about one and a half hours to set up on special track.

(d) This late model 400-mm. howitzer was typical of the more complicated heavy equipments. It was fired from a specially constructed firing platform which took all the weight off the rail wheels and required 12 hours to build. It had an arc of fire of only 12° across the centre line.

35 370-mm. gun on rail mounting (France)

Those unfamiliar with the metric system of measurement may not at first realise the full massiveness of the heavier railway guns, or their destructive capabilities. Perhaps this view of one of the heaviest weapons used by either side will give a better impression of what mounting these huge pieces involved. This particular one is a 370-mm. naval gun equivalent in calibre and power to an English 15-in. gun of the type normally mounted only in the heaviest warships. As with certain other examples of railway artillery, the barrel was actually a smaller calibre weapon bored out to size; in this case the original was a 305-mm. weapon. It was mounted on two 4-axle bogies each with an axle load of 20 tonnes, a precaution needed since some of these big guns on their mountings weighed in excess of 150 tons. The carriage was fitted with a recoil recuperation system which, linked to recuperators on the gun mount itself, enabled the weapon to be used from any firing curve without special track preparation. The actual mounting was pivoted and the gun had an arc of fire 6° each side of the track centre line. Rate of fire was theoretically one round every three minutes and a $\frac{1}{2}$ ton shell could be fired over a maximum range of nearly $16\frac{1}{2}$ km.—just over 10 miles.

36 320-mm. rail-borne cannon (France)

This shows a typical A.L.V.F. piece, a 320-mm. ex-coastal defence gun in firing position on what was known as an 'epi' (lit: sword) or firing curve. The principle was the same as in the British Boer War artillery; the gun could not be fired more than a few degrees each side of the railway centre line so it was installed on a specially built curved siding along which it could be shunted to provide a different arc of fire. The '320' was a rigidly mounted weapon employing the 'glissement' principle to absorb recoil. In this case the rearward motion was absorbed by braked wheels or shoes running on longitudinal guides on each side of the track. The weapon took one and a half hours to set up on an already laid epi and could theoretically fire at a rate of one shell every few minutes.

37 240-mm. T.R. gun on 60-cm. gauge trucks (France)

Almost incredibly, guns of calibres as large as 240-mm. could be hauled by the 60-cm. gauge artillery railways. This shows the method of carrying the specially adapted 240-T.R. weapon (Schneider, le Creusot) on special 6-wheeled bolster wagons. The barrel went on two trucks and the massive mount (affut) on two others with trunnion sockets uppermost. Needless to say the gun could not be fired from the 60-cm. gauge in this condition nor could any heavier artillery although long 120-mm. and short 155-mm. pieces were carried complete on special trucks.

38 240-mm. T.R. gun on 60-cm. gauge (France)

The older models of 240-mm. gun used by the French artillery could not only be transported over the 60-cm. gauge tracks but, when mounted on special trucks, could be fired from it. These trucks were massive girder-frame affairs mounted on two, 6-wheeled bogies and were apparently gauge-convertible (standard gauge buffers and drawgear were fitted). The gun was rigidly mounted and the truck was jacked up onto sleepers when firing was to take place.

39 12-in. howitzer on rail truck (U.K.)

France was not the only country to produce specialist railway guns. Most of the heavy British howitzers were at one time or another mounted on rail trucks and a typical fitting was the standard 12-in. howitzer shown here. Unlike most of World War One railway guns this was capable of a 360° traverse and its mountings show signs of direct descent from the 6-in. rail-borne artillery of the Boer War. It was self-contained and capable of being fired from unprepared track. Hydraulically actuated sponsons with adjustable feet were simply swung out on each side of the track and locked into position. The gun itself had a recuperator, and springs took the remainder of the recoil.

40 12-in. Mk IX gun on rail mounting (U.K.)

Typical of the heavier long barrel guns operated by the British was this 12-in. Mark IX weapon operated during the Somme battle in 1916. Both the Royal Garrison Artillery and the Royal Marine Artillery operated the heavy weapons and this R.G.A. one shows features common to many. In particular note the massive bogies—with what amounts to a match-truck at the front—the girder frames to support the main gun-trunnions, and the framed canvas and metal cover over the rear portion where shells were brought up for loading. The gun is shown here in travelling condition but could be fired from any suitably curved stretch of track; unlike the French equivalents it was mounted high enough for the breech to clear the ground at full recoil when at firing elevation.

41 28-cm. long barrelled gun (Germany)

Very similar in general concept to the British guns is this typical German weapon, a 28-cm. cannon. The bogies appear to be made from old locomotive frames and wheels, and it displays the same pattern of deep girder framing to support the weapon weight. Quite normal for German guns was the

shrapnel-proof iron sheeting over the ammunition loading bay; it should perhaps be explained that these guns did not normally carry their own shells. These were stored in a van at the rear and carried up to the breech by some form of hoist, very much as in naval practice. The canvas awning shown is a camouflage and weather cover to drape over the barrel.

42 30-cm. captured railway gun (Germany)

Displaying all the main features of such guns is this 30-cm. German weapon captured by the Australians late in 1918. These big guns were extremely vulnerable to a sudden advance since it took some time to make them ready for travelling; in addition they could be easily 'bottled up' by a break in the track or, as happened on more than one occasion, a lucky shell landing on their locomotive. Their captors were always disproportionally proud! This one shown clearly the bogie mountings, the heavy girder frames and the rear shell-hoist. As was common in German practice, the protective roof and side shielding was of metal plate where allied weapons normally used removable canvas awnings.

SPECIAL V.I.P. TRAINS AND COACHES 1914-18

Most senior commanders on both sides in the European land conflict had either special trains or special coaches to act as mobile headquarters; one railway coach even played a vital part in the final surrender for it was at Marshal Foch's train headquarters at Compiègne that the

Armistice was signed in November, 1918. It might be considered an unnecessary extravagance for such sets of vehicles to be made available but they did allow the commanders to move complete staffs from one end of the front to the other without the disruption of dismantling and setting up a static headquarters.

43/45 Layout of special train for C-in-C (U.K.)

To describe all such trains would be ridiculous but these plates show the detailed layout of one—the train of Sir Douglas Haig, the British Commander-in-Chief—together with views of typical vehicles. This train was requested in April, 1917, the London & North Western Railway being asked to provide, first, ten vehicles, and then a few months later an additional four. As can be seen from a glance at the diagram, the coaches had to provide both working and living accommodation; fortunately the company had available several examples of that splendid Edwardian institution the picnic salon, rendered redundant by the war. These, to a standard 42 ft by 8 ft 6-in. design, were easily adaptable, the arrangement of doors and windows being very convenient and they formed the basis of the train: only the two stores vehicles (fitted up from full brakes) and the telephone exchange were different. The detail diagrams (Plates 43/44) show the train as originally sent out; it was remarshalled at various times during its career but individual vehicles were not altered. The train comprised:

1. A complete coach for the C-in-C, comprising a bathroom, bedroom and rather spartan sitting room—though he did have the distinction of having curtains in his bedroom in addition to the normal blinds.

2. A coach for the personal aide who had a 'bathroomette', a bedroom and an office where his immediate staff worked. Oddly enough neither the C-in-C nor his aide appear to have had a lavatory, although every other living coach was so equipped!

3-7. Coaches for the senior staff offices, 3-5 each comprising either three bedrooms or two bedrooms and an office, together with baths and lavatories. No. 6 had a single bedroom and a general purpose room used as an annexe to coach 7 which was termed the officers' mess. It was in effect a dining room and serving pantry.

8. The kitchen car which also housed the lighting plant and stores.

9-10. Living coaches for the other ranks who staffed the train and acted as servants, clerks, etc. They were accommodated in two-or four-bedded rooms and had their own mess.

11-12. No. 11 was a general office with a room for the Senior N.C.O. in charge of the clerks and 12 a mobile telephone exchange linked to all major rooms in the train and capable of being linked with outside networks at short notice. The train was completed by two rather longer full-brake vehicles which were used as stores (Plate 45). One of these also contained a steam heating plant for heating the train when it was not attached to a locomotive. The whole train was linked by corridor connections and formed an efficient and comfortable headquarters for short periods; it was normally used only for such periods since G.H.Q. was permanently established at a Château some way behind the lines.

46 Special sleeper for Premier Clemenceau (France)

During the years 1917–18, two special coaches were provided for the French Prime Minister, Georges Clemenceau. Both were originally standard bogie vehicles of the Compagnie Internationale des Wagons-Lits, a sleeping saloon No. 2444 and a restaurant car, No. 2426. The plan of 2444 shows how it was fitted up for Clemenceau and his immediate staff. The premier himself had a suite of three rooms, comprising bedroom, bathroom and dressing room with an office-cum-sitting room adjoining. Staff accommodation, presumably for his aide and immediate servants was more spartan.

STANDARD GAUGE FREIGHT ROLLING-STOCK (U.K.)

Partly because of its length, partly because of its static nature, World War One was the first war in which railways were used so extensively that civilian rolling stock proved insufficient. It was always intended by the major powers that, in the event of war, civilian railways would simply be requisitioned; since the art of bombing was in its infancy and most main lines were out of shell-range, it was thought that the normal railway resources could deal with the traffic.

In practice, the fantastic requirements of supplying huge armies in static trench lines made this task impossible for the existing railways and all countries supplied new stock, usually on

very traditional lines. Perhaps the most odd result was that shown by the vehicles ordered from British firms by the British War Department; British practice had long differed from that of the Continent and the conflict of ideas produced some very surprising results.

47 10-ton 4-wheeled goods van

The typical goods vehicle on all British railways in the 1914 period was the 10–12-ton capacity, short wheelbase wagon and van. Like the example here, built by the Midland Railway Carriage & Wagon Co., it had no train brakes and was very much a single purpose vehicle; livestock had special cattle wagons, goods of different descriptions had their own particular pattern of vehicle. To start with the War Department simply ordered these since it was, presumably, accustomed to them.

48 20-ton 4-wheeled open wagon

First innovation was the production of larger vehicles to match continental practice. This 20-ton capacity open wagon by the Gloucester Railway Carriage & Wagon Co., built for war use in 1917, shows the bigger load area and long wheelbase. It is interesting to note that in contrast to the 60-cm. gauge rolling-stock, even this design was surprisingly inefficient, whereas a 60-cm. gauge wagon of 10-tons capacity had a tare weight of between 2 and 3 tons, this wagon tared 8 tons 11 cwt—almost half as much as its load capacity.

49 25-ton brake van

Unbraked wagons have to have separate brake-vans. The 'standard' W.D. 25-ton van was in fact a conversion from the 'A' type 20-ton covered wagon built by the firm of Stableford & Co. at Coalville. Such firms were usually very proud of their contribution to the war effort and this works photograph in shop grey, testifies to the achievement of its builders McLellan's of Glasgow.

50   Continental pattern 20-ton goods van

For once the British were out of step. The pattern of covered goods vehicle used by all the belligerent continental powers was a multi-purpose vehicle. As well as having a high capacity and long wheelbase, features due largely to continental conditions, it could be used both for livestock and for carriage of either perishable or non-perishable goods. The feature that allowed this was the set of metal ventilating flaps along the upper part of each side. When in place the van was waterproof; when they were lowered by means of the straps below them, they revealed mesh-covered grilles which let in air and light. Another feature was that a proportion of all wagons and vans were braked, not just by lever-operated parking brakes but by screw brakes operated by brakesmen sitting in perches. These were so sited as to allow the brakesman a view along the train, but gave him little weather protection.

Faced with these odd continental practices, the British compromised. They produced some short and some long wheelbase vehicles and stuck brakesmen's huts on them—which they erroneously called cabooses. The early placings of these—with no view but more comfort than the average continental ones—

may have been influenced by thoughts of the restricted British loading gauge.

51   20-ton goods van with brakesman's perch

This 20-ton goods van was a typical timber-framed vehicle of the period as running on several British railways, with its diagonal-strutted panels and single sliding door on each side. The bodywork was simply shifted along slightly and a crude hut built onto one end with a 'bay window' to accommodate the pillar brake wheel. Either the War Department had not grasped the principle that brakesmen should be able to look along the train or they expected them to operate by whistle codes. The vehicles were built by the Birmingham Railway Carriage & Wagon Co., during 1917–18.

52   12-ton wagon with brakesman's perch

Another illustration of incomprehension is this ordinary 12-ton open wagon by Charles Roberts & Co. of Horbury, with a brakesman's seat on extended underframe at one end. If the man sat to shelter from the weather, he could neither see along the train nor effectively operate the high brake wheel. If he stood up to do so, he was completely unprotected.

53   End views of wagon and van

This shows end views of the two wagons described above to illustrate the deliberately squat nature of the brakesmen's perches.

54 10-ton high-sided wagon

A more rational answer was this 10-ton open high-sided wagon produced by the Gloucester Railway Carriage & Wagon Co. during 1917–18. A normal, two-door vehicle it had a slightly shortened and offset body, with a proper brakesman's hut at one end. This was both enclosed and set high enough for the brakesman to see along a train of wagons.

55 Low-sided wagons with and without brake huts

In some instances it would appear that existing continental designs were used or were modified. This series of views shows a typical low-sided 16–20-ton wagon built in quantity for the War Office and destined specifically for service on main lines in France. The vehicles were even sent out in the appropriate railway livery—in this case the État (State) railway working between Paris and Le Havre—and bore the appropriate wagon data. This set of wagons was built by the Metropolitan Carriage Wagon & Finance Co. and shows clearly the difference caused by the addition of a proper brakesman's hut.

STANDARD GAUGE LOCOMOTIVES (U.S.A.)

56 Baldwin 2-8-0 freight locomotive

In 1916, the need for standard gauge locomotives was great and, as frequently happened, orders were placed in the United States for a 2-cylinder simple expansion locomotive, 150 being supplied for R.O.D. use within a year. The design was considered so successful

that it was adopted as standard by the U.S. Army when the United States entered the war. The American variant, commonly known as the 'Pershing's' after the American Commander-in-Chief, differed only in being superheated and no less than 1946 were built between July, 1917 and November, 1918; at one time they were arriving in France at the rate of 300 a month. Leading dimensions were: boiler pressure to 190 lb/sq in.; cylinders 21 in. by 28 in.; coupled wheel diameter 4 ft 8 in.

57 Baldwin 4-6-0 mixed traffic locomotive

The British also ordered various other types of locomotive, both large and small from the seemingly inexhaustible Baldwin Co. during 1916 and 1917. Not prominent but none the less probably the most pleasing to look at was a series of mixed traffic 4-6-0s ordered—and delivered—in 1917. Presumably the R.O.D. felt the need for locomotives suitable for working passenger trains to reasonably fast timings. The locomotives followed traditional American practice with high-set boilers, bar frames and commodious cabs but none the less somehow contrived to look handsome.

DEVELOPMENT OF FIELD RAILWAYS

Standard gauge railways rapidly proved insufficient for forward area supply, both on the Western and on the Eastern and Italian Fronts. The static war with its extensive trench lines soon produced a wide 'battle zone' in which the ground was so shell-torn and fought over that bad weather made it almost impassable. Hence, for the last two or three miles supplies and men had to be laboriously brought up on foot. As a result, all the major combatants rapidly developed some form of tactical field railway to improve their communications with the front line. As usual the Germans had thought it out well in advance and were able to put their South West African experience to good use; they already had standardised 60-cm. gauge equipment in vast quantities and a network of light railways soon grew up behind their front line. The French, too, reacted quickly. They had for some years been using 60-cm. gauge railways in fortified areas to serve the fortress artillery, and these were quickly developed and expanded. The British, typically, were initially caught completely unprepared and took a long time to conform; but by the end, again typically, they had probably the best system of all.

The British problem was that, with the Boer War in mind, its commanders believed that a war of movement would break out at any moment and that light railways were therefore unnecessary. Apart from isolated locally-built 'trench tramways' they did not take tactical railway communication seriously until late 1916 but from then on their railway web proliferated exceedingly fast. In France alone over 1000 km. were in use by the war's end, with more than 700 steam locomotives and over a thousand petrol tractors. Again they were on the 60 cm. gauge, although this was chosen mainly to conform with the French—previously the 2 ft 6 in. (760 mm.) gauge had been regarded as the ideal for what were then termed 'siege railways'.

These field railways on both sides produced some of the most interesting railway equipment ever used by the military and the following pages portray both them and it.

RAILWAYS IN THE FRONT LINE

58 Improvised trolley for transporting wounded (U.K.)

The light railways, proper, finished some four or five hundred yards behind the actual front line for fear of damage by shelling; in front of them were the trench tramways, crude and lightly laid tracks using rail weighing only 9 lb/yd, and suitable only for horse or man-haulage. Often blown up, frequently patched together again, sometimes even with wooden rails, these were nevertheless extremely valuable. They carried up supplies and ammunition, and brought back the wounded, saving them an agonising journey plodding through mud. The improvised trolleys like that shown here, were at first built locally in corps workshops or even on site and were quickly fitted with end bars to allow stretchers to be carried as well as the so-called 'walking wounded'. They were extremely simple, having no springing at all and the ride over rickety track must have been bone-shaking.

59 'P' class dual purpose wagon for wounded (U.K.)

British ingenuity eventually came to the rescue, in the shape of a small 4-wheeled wagon capable of running both in light railway trains and on trench tramways. This, the 'P' class wagon (fully described on Plate 123) had sprung axleboxes and could be quickly adapted to carry either stores or stretchers. Special ends were provided to allow for two tiers of

123

stretcher cases—four in all—and the wagons often ran with a 'mixture' of fittings. This, having brought up stores—hence the slatted sides—is now conveying wounded back to a casualty clearing station.

MONORAIL AND SUSPENSION DEVICES (U.K.)

In a number of front-line areas, even the light and fairly easily dismantlable trench tramways could not be used—sometimes because of the danger of exposure to the enemy, sometimes because they had to run in communication trenches, sometimes because the ground to be traversed was too shell-torn to be formed easily into a trackbed. A partial solution was found in the use of single (mono) rail systems and in aerial ropeways.

60 Standard monorail truck for man haulage

The 'official' solution was a ground-level monorail consisting simply of 9 lb/yd rail spiked down to short sleeper blocks and laid alongside a path. On this ran a small truck rather similar to the 'P' class in having a flat body with removable slatted sides, and fixed slatted ends. It differed from other trucks in having not a conventional underframe but a braced structure which extended beyond each end just off the centre line and supported wheels in tandem. At one end, also, vertical supports held a horizontal piece of gas-piping at chest height, this being grasped by the operator and used both to balance and propel the car. Stability at rest was ensured by small skids at each side.

The system had the advantages of being simple to construct and almost indistinguishable from the air, but needed reasonably level ground; it was used fairly widely, some 1404 trucks being supplied to the Western Front.

61 Irish pattern monorail

This was a 'field' design conceived by one Captain Finnimore R.E. to enable trench lines to traverse badly torn-up ground. It was in essence a simple version of the French Lartigue system using balanced panniers hung each side of a raised central rail but without the Lartigue's guide rails—which it did not apparently miss. The single car 'train' could take up to 400 lb of cargo and was used mainly for removing 'spoil' from trenches. Construction was simple, utilising a 9 lb/yd rail spiked direct on to vertical posts, and hand, cable and even motor-worked versions were produced. The plate shows one of the latter—perhaps the only one—apparently propelled by a motor-cycle engine. The name, incidentally, came obviously from recollections of the Irish Listowel & Ballybunion Railway that had been built to the Lartigue system a few years before.

62 Wilson monorail for trench use

This was another field device in which Captain Finnimore again had a hand. It was specifically designed for moving wounded and stores in confined trenches where conventional railways would cause obstruction, and consisted of a flat 'rail' hung from cross beams and supporting a tray suspended from double-flanged wheels in tandem. It could carry about 200 lb but was really useful only in deep communication trenches where there were no zig-zags or sharp corners; this somewhat naturally restricted its use to one or two rear areas!

63 Aerial ropeway

Although not really *railways* these were occasionally used as tramway substitutes and both the Leeming and Hamilton systems were used. As can be seen from the aerial ropeway shown here, they were conventional suspension lines with fixed 'dollies' clipped on to carrier ropes.

EARLY PETROL TRACTORS

64 The 'Scotch Express' (U.K.)

Improvisation was a feature especially of the British and, as the primitive trench tramways grew longer and more complex, man and mule haulage became insufficient. Hence front-line units evolved a weird and wonderful assortment of petrol-driven 'devices' made up from bits and pieces scrounged from all over the place. This shows a typical production, the 'Scotch Express' which was famous over a wide area, although mainly for its headboard! That was probably the most efficient thing about it, the remainder being composed of a trolley frame with an old De Dion engine and gearbox driving on one axle. Haulage power was virtually nil.

65 McEwan Pratt 10-h.p. tractor (U.K.)

Typically British, too, was the thought that since these ramshackle lines existed

it was better to try and find locomotives to run on them rather than relay the lot properly. The first result was the so-called McEwan Pratt tractor, in effect a standard design of E. E. Baguley Ltd. but built by a subsidiary firm. Two of these peculiar little machines were ordered for trials in 1916 but proved underpowered and tricky to handle so were rejected for trench-work. None the less the Inspectorate of Iron Structures—imposing name!—found them useful for trundling items round the sharp curves of base workshops and 50 were ordered. Plate 65 shows one on typical duty lugging a tank engine around. Loaded weight was just under 2 tons and they had a 2-cylinder water-cooled petrol engine.

66 McEwan Pratt 10-h.p. tractor with cab

This plate shows the McEwan Pratt machine as originally ordered; it is interesting to note the extremely small space taken up by the little petrol engine. The 'weather canopy' was optional but can have provided little protection to the driver unless the rail was falling vertically or the sun was at the zenith.

67 Early Ford car on rails (U.K.)

Naturally enough, attempts were made to convert road motors to run on rails in a more satisfactory manner than the 'Scotch Express' ever did. One fairly workman-like conversion was this early-pattern Ford Model T. The complete chassis including transmission and rear axle was mounted permanently on a simple underframe, the original drive being transferred to rail wheels by means of chains and sprockets. To judge from the pile of sandbags dumped on the rear 'tray', adhesion was not as good as it might have been! This conversion can be considered a forerunner of the slightly more sophisticated Crewe tractors (Plates 68/69) although it was not convertible from rail to road or vice versa.

68/69 Crewe tractor (U.K.)

Another British improvisation, the Crewe tractor had its unlikely genesis in the London & North Western Railway Works after which it was named. Legend has it that the C.M.E.'s daughter 'while entertaining an officer on leave in Paris' dreamed up the idea of a light convertible tractor easily improvised from available parts. Or, to put it more poetically as the official history did, she 'devised a scheme whereby the vehicle, remaining self-contained, was both convertible and reconvertible; that is to say, like the hare it could speed along the high road to any given point or locality where, quickly transformed, it would, like the tortoise, commence its slower and uneven progress on a diminutive line of rails, laid haphazard across some devastated area, unballasted, lop-sided, up and down, this way and that way'.

Crewe realised the vision by simply taking the chassis of a standard Ford Model T motor-car and so modifying it that the road wheels could be quickly replaced with rail wheels in a plate underframe with chain drive from the Ford rear axle; the plates show the device in 'road' and 'rail' mode. Drive arrangements were necessarily crude; after much cogitation Crewe decided that optimum speed for the Ford trans-mission was 25 m.p.h. and they reduced this by about half through gearing for rail use. There was no reverse gear but they proudly installed a built-in turning plate to 'allow the vehicle to be turned round at any point'. Confident in L.N.W. workmanship even over such an unlikely production, the Crewe engineers even guaranteed a haulage capacity of 5 tons on a 1 in 20 gradient. Alas, even Jove nods! In spite of all the poetic descriptions the august Crewe works could not really envisage its products using any tracks less than of L.N.W. standard; thus the test track was laid immaculately and in 'front line' conditions the claimed performance often became almost non-existent.

Nor was the convertible feature much used; the machines were officially 'Motor Transport' property but once acquired by a tramway unit they were 'lost' to the road for good.

70 Rail motor lorry (Austria)

The British on the Western Front were not the only combatants to put road vehicles on rails. In Russia and on the Italian Front the Military Railways Department of the Imperial Austro-Hungarian Army also found the idea useful for rapid transport over lightly laid lines in difficult country; not much information is available about the subject of this painting but it is obviously a standard army lorry of the period simply converted for standard gauge by replacing the road wheels with flanged ones; the chain drive was probably original. Of note, however, is the railway-type coupling which suggests that it could be used either 'in multiple' or to haul light trailers.

71 **Ford rail motor lorry** (East Africa)

Possibly inspired by the Crewe tractors, the British Indian Army once more turned to the products of Henry Ford for the East African campaign of 1917–18. There, as the wily Count von Lettow Worbeck withdrew into Central Africa, the British communications got longer and longer: For some time almost the only viable link was a former rickety plantation railway of 60-cm. gauge which had been extended westwards from the so-called 'harbour' of Lindi. It could not withstand even light steam locomotives and the problem was only solved by commandeering some M.T. department Ford Model T 1-ton lorries and mounting them on rail wheels. The conversion was simple, a crude bogie replacing the front axle while steel flanged wheels were pressed straight on to the original Ford rear axle. The result, once the Ford suspension had been suitably strengthened to stop axle breakages, was effective and the vehicles even towed light trailers.

PUGS (60-cm. gauge) 1914–18

Trench tramways, however, were only the last link in the distribution system. Much more important were the true tactical light railways. Every army had light 4- or 6-wheeled locomotives for shunting base areas on their tactical light railways. Typical were the two British designs; slightly less typical was one produced for the French.

72/74 **Hudson 0-6-0WT** (U.K.)

The first steam locomotives used on British Western Front light railways were a class of 0-6-0 well tanks supplied by the well-known firm of R. Husdon Ltd. They were actually built by Messrs. Hudswell Clarke Ltd. under sub-contract but are always known as 'Hudsons' or 'pugs' (generic nickname for a short-wheelbase shunter). These were conventional industrial machines used from early 1916 on, and 58 in all saw service, at least one even gaining a 'wound stripe' for damage on active service by enemy fire! Leading dimensions were: cylinders 6½ in. by 12 in.; boiler pressure 180 lb/sq in.; weight in working order 6·98 tons; wheelbase 4 ft 2 in.; wheel diameter 1 ft 11 in.

73/74 **Barclay 0-6-0WT** (U.K.)

Twenty-five of these were ordered during 1916, being an adaptation of the makers standard 'F' class design. Produced by the Scottish firm of Andrew Barclay Ltd., they appear to have been used almost exclusively by the Australians, and no other class of Allied or Axis locomotive was so little photographed! Leading dimensions were: cylinders 6¾ in. by 10¾ in.; boiler pressure 160 lb/sq in.; weight in working order 6⅜ tons; wheelbase 4 ft 4 in.; wheel diameter 1 ft 10 in.

75 **Baldwin 0-6-0ST** (U.S.A. for France)

In somewhat striking contrast to the angular British designs was this typically American 0-6-0ST, a hundred of which were produced for the French Government Artillery Railways in 1916. Like most 60-cm. gauge steam locomotives it was of simple—although rather low-slung—design and was fitted with a water lifter to enable it to take water from any source. Notable are the full cab and the direct, external sandpipes to the front and rear wheels. The large spark arrester was fitted since it had to work among live ammunition and other explosive stores. Leading dimensions were: cylinders 9 in. by 12 in. and coupled wheels of 26 in. diameter.

VARIATIONS ON A THEME— (60-cm. gauge) 'MAIN LINE' STEAM

All the combatants in World War One needed fairly powerful locomotives for 'main-line' haulage on their light railway systems; typical requirement was for haulage of 50 tons up to a *1 in 50* gradient or six loaded bogie wagons (about 70 tons in all) along the level. The French and Germans already had such machines at the outbreak of war, the others had to evolve their own.

76 Pechot 0-4-4-0T (France)

Oldest design was that evolved by Messrs. Pechot and Bourdon for French artillery railways in 1882. The requirements of hauling heavy artillery pieces (Plate 37) and the very sharp curves found in early fortress railways led to an articulated locomotive that was really a variant of the Fairlie design. It had a rigid frame carrying the cab, side tanks and boilers, mounted on two flexibly connected power bogies. Unlike the Fairlies it had only one firebox, operated from one side of the central cab and with a single massive steam dome mounted directly above it; the huge spark arresters were intended to prevent 'firework displays' giving away its position at night

and to allow working in close proximity to artillery explosive stores. The Pechot, built mainly by Franco-Belge at Raismes, was the standard major locomotive well before World War One and was so highly thought of that a further 280 were built during it, 100 by the North British Locomotive Company and 180 by Baldwin's in America. The locomotives were very strong but rather delicate and were used mainly in rear areas on fairly good track.

77 Feldbahn 0-8-0T (Germany)

Like the French, the Germans developed their military light railway locomotives during the last two decades of the 19th century but in their case mainly for military field railways and colonial lines. They eventually standardised on a neat 0-8-0T which was built in very large quantities by at least eleven makers, over 2500 being produced up to 1919. These locomotives varied in detail but were essentially very similar, and well adapted for light railway working with excellent adhesion and a comparatively roomy cab having a dropped floor to enable enginemen to stand upright. The long wheelbase necessitated by 8-coupled wheels was made flexible by use of Klien-Lindner axles front and rear (Plate 9). These, strongly reminiscent of Sir Arthur Heywood's contemporary design for 15 in. gauge, allowed a degree of lateral and swivel play while retaining fairly rigid coupling rods. Like the Pechots, some machines were fitted with big spark-arresting chimneys of the continental flat-topped pattern. A typical locomotive had 2 cylinders 240-mm. diameter and 240-mm. stroke, a boiler pressure of 215 lb/sq in. and weight in working order of nearly 12½ tons. Coupled wheel diameter was 590 mm. and total wheelbase 2260 mm., though the rigid wheelbase was 790 mm. only.

78   Hunslet 4-6-0T (U.K.)

The British, who had to start from scratch in 1915, took a different line of development. They envisaged simply enlarging their current 6-coupled designs and carrying the extra weight on idler wheels as was common on British light railways of the period. The choice of a 4-6-0T was to some extent fortuitous, caused by (i) the current practice of turning tank locomotives at each end of their journey, so that a leading bogie which gave the best weight distribution was acceptable, and (ii) the fact that Hunslet's had an existing 0-6-0T design of suitable power readily adaptable to a 4-6-0 configuration.

The result was the very neat and typically British locomotive pictured here, of which about 100 in all saw service. It was strong, well-balanced and much coveted by the light railway troops whose only complaint was that Hunslet could not produce enough. It had features common to all later Allied light railway locomotives, these including 'bumper bars' fore and aft to ensure engines did not derail too thoroughly; massive rerailing jacks with built-in jacking points; and a water-lifter to enable water to be taken from shell-holes and other unusual sources in an emergency. Leading dimensions included cylinders 9½ in. by 10¾ in., boiler pressure of 160 lb/sq in., a coupled wheelbase of 5 ft 6 in. and driving wheels 2 ft in diameter. Weight in working order was just over 14 tons.

79   Baldwin 4-6-0T (U.S.A. for U.K.)

Quite the most common allied locomotive was the 4-6-0T design produced in quantity by Baldwin Locomotive Co. for the War Department when it was found that Hunslet production capacity was insufficient. By coincidence Baldwins, when approached in 1916, already had a 4-6-0T design closely approximating to the British specification and, with slight modifications, turned out no less than 495 between March, 1916 and April, 1917.

These machines were the mainstay of the British light railway effort although they were never as popular as the Hunslets. Rather ungainly with a high centre of gravity, and mass-produced for a short life to lower tolerances than the hand-built British machines, they were rough riders and had a tendency to derail. In particular they proved that the 4-6-0T layout was far from ideal particularly where much bunker-first running was inevitable. None the less they were rugged and had the advantage that parts were easily interchangeable between members of the class; they were used extensively on all fronts except East Africa.

Leading dimensions were: cylinders (2) 9 in. by 12 in.; boiler pressure 178 lb/sq in.; coupled wheelbase 5 ft 8 in.; coupled wheel diameter 1 ft 11½ in. Weight in working order was 14½ tons.

80   ALCO 2-6-2T (U.S.A. for U.K.)

By late 1916, the shortcomings of the 4-6-0T design were becoming apparent and when tenders were invented for further machines, the American Locomotive Company suggested a 2-6-2T design. One hundred were promptly ordered, materialising as handsome, typically American side-tank locomotives fairly similar in appearance to the Baldwins. Although the biggest light railway engines produced for the British, they were nevertheless so well balanced that axle-loading was still well within the specified limits, and they appear to have been strong and well liked by their crews. The trailing truck certainly cut down derailments and their main fault was the still high centre of gravity, which made them somewhat unstable on rough track. Leading dimensions were: cylinders 9 in. by 14 in.; boiler pressure 175 lb/sq in.; coupled wheelbase 5 ft 6 in.; coupled wheel diameter 2 ft 3 in. Weight in working order was a little over 17 tons.

81 Baldwin 2-6-2T (U.S.A.)

The Americans, coming into the war late, were the last combatants to acquire light railways but they did have the advantage of being able to standardise from the start, building on other people's experience. Thus their standard steam locomotive was an all-purpose machine, designed by Baldwins as a double-ended version of their earlier 4-6-0T. Apart from the more sensible wheel arrangement and a lowered centre of gravity, it was very similar to its predecessor and some hundreds were produced for the U.S. Army. A good many of these went overseas in support of the American Expeditionary Force but numbers also served at bases within the United States.

VARIATIONS ON VARIATIONS
(60-cm. gauge)

82 Baldwin 4-6-0T under repair

Many of the light railway locomotives used by both sides received modifications in the field at various times in their careers—and often borrowed parts from sister locomotives of the same class. The reason was often the primitiveness of repair facilities available in the field, which led to cannibalisation of damaged machines when replacements were urgently needed. This Baldwin 4-6-0T is on a typical open-air servicing track, simply a section of track raised a little above the ground for convenience of working. The blank space on her side-tank indicates that she has either acquired a neighbour's tank or that she is in the throes of a renumbering scheme that occurred during 1917.

83 Hunslet 4-6-0T with condensing gear

When light railways came into serious use the problem immediately arose of how to conceal movement of trains; steam locomotives in forward areas often gave themselves away through the smoke and steam. The British War Department decided to experiment with condensing gear as fitted to underground trains and the last of an order for 75 Hunslet 4-6-0T (see Plate 78) was so fitted. Unfortunately conversion was rather slow and by the time when it appeared, in mid-1917, satisfactory petrol-engined tractors had been developed which could do the job even more inconspicuously. Therefore, although the condensing gear worked satisfactorily, it was not proceeded with and 375 remained a solitary example.

PICKING UP WATER (60-cm. gauge)

Steam locomotives propel themselves by turning water into steam and, hence, require a constant supply of water if they are to function at all. The provision of this on the tactical light railways of World War One was always a considerable headache, except in the quieter back areas; there normal railway facilities could be provided. In more exposed areas, and on lines whose route altered from time to time for tactical reasons, more esoteric methods had to be employed. There are gruesome tales of locomotives held up by shelling or other mishaps which only got home because their crews boiled water from shell holes with their tin helmets! As experience grew, however, four major methods of watering came to be employed.

84 Taking water via a water lifter (Allied)

The most basic was the original shell-hole method 'modernised'. As soon as the problem was fully realised, both sides fitted their locomotives with so-called water lifters. These were a species of injector-cum-pump designed to suck water in from an outside source below tank level and then to squirt it through what looked like a lavatory overflow pipe into a side-tank—usually the left-hand one. The business-end of the machine was mounted either below or just in front of the cab, the inlet nozzle normally being sited centrally on the rear buffer-beam; this enabled water to be taken from the left or right side with

equal facility. Apart from the outlet pipe to a side-tank, the apparatus was not prominent but locomotives thus fitted are easily recognisable. They usually carried lengths of flexible large diameter hose, draped over steel rests either on the side tanks (French) or on the cab rear (British and German).

Slightly more respectable (and much better for the boiler) was the use of a mobile water tank such as those shown in Plates 89/90. These could be filled with clean, softened water and run on to a convenient siding near the current base of operations; the water lifter was, of course, still required for transferring the precious fluid.

When things became more permanent, large galvanised-iron tanks were often constructed using a brick or sleeper base. They were filled either from a well or via a motor-driven pump but were rarely very high. Hence the ubiquitous water lifter again came into its own, as seen here.

85 Auxiliary water tender (Germany)

The Germans, as usual, had foreseen the problem beforehand. Not only were Feldbahn locomotives fitted with water lifters from the start, they could also be equipped with auxiliary bogie tenders with direct hose connections to the locomotive injectors. These tenders were originally developed for colonial use but were widely used on longer runs everywhere. Their advantages were constant supply of water and coal; the disadvantage was that the locomotive was pulling non-productive deadweight; this could even include extra men, seats for two 'guards' being provided fore and aft.

TOO MUCH WATER IN THE WRONG PLACE (60-cm. gauge)

86/87 Events leading to derailment by water

The engineman's troubles were by no means over when he had managed to take on enough water to make steam. Peculiar to the American-built steam-engines with their high-set tanks was what happened to that water on uncertain track. The tanks of the Baldwins and ALCOs were joined underneath by a link pipe to equalise the water drawn off—a fine idea in theory and one shared by other types but one which was frequently embarrassing for these particular locomotives owing to their high centre of gravity. Plate 86 shows what would happen if the locomotive stood for any time on a slanted piece of track with half-empty tanks. The water ran 'down-hill' from one to the other; as the 'lower' tank filled, so the distribution of weight made the locomotive unstable and eventually it toppled over on to its side (Plate 87). It was not unknown for this to happen to Feldbahn and Hunslet machines but the occurrence was much less frequent.

88 Using an improvised tender

In desperation a number of American tank engines were 'converted' to tender engines by the simple expedient of removing their tanks, putting them on a four-wheeled flat wagon, and arranging a connection to the locomotive injectors; the operation was comparatively simple since the tanks simply rested on flat trays, being held in position by yokes across the boiler. Needless to say, how-

ever, the enginemen's troubles did not stop there and there are many sad stories of drivers on a dark night putting on their injectors only to find that the 'tender' had become detached, all unnoticed in the darkness. It might be noted that a number of other locomotives were similarly treated after the war but mainly to reduce their axle-loading.

CARRYING LIQUID IN BULK

89 'H' class bogie tank wagon (U.K.)

All combatants using the 60-cm. gauge during World War One at some time found themselves having to use large capacity tank wagons to supply water—both to troops and for railway purposes. Typical of the special purpose vehicles developed to meet this need was the British 'H' class tank wagon. This was simply a standard bogie wagon underframe as used on the 'D' class open goods wagon, fitted with a 1500 (imperial) gallon capacity tank. The tank had a manhole at each end but, unlike very similar continental vehicles, no hand-pump was provided.

90 Standard bogie tank wagon (U.S.A.)

The U.S. equivalent is shown here to illustrate the close similarities between wagons. It is not perhaps so surprising in this case since the Americans designed their standard equipment at a late stage of the war and modelled them largely on existing British and French designs. Typical of the American attitude towards large scale planning is the fact that no less than 166 of these specialised vehicles were sent to France during the short period in which the Americans were engaged.

CARRYING LIQUID IN BULK: IMPROVISATIONS

There were various occasions on which the large tank wagons had far too great a capacity, or on which small quantities of several different liquids were required simultaneously. To meet this need both the French and the British improvised multi-cargo wagons.

91 'G' class 4-wheeled tank wagon (U.K.)

This vehicle was produced in small numbers, mainly for supplying tractors 'on detachment' from their main base. It was built up on an early pattern 4-wheeled wagon underframe on which was mounted three upright rectangular tanks, each with a capacity of 180 gallons. One carried paraffin, one lubricating oil and one cylinder oil, their respective contents were clearly indicated in stencilled lettering. Length was 8 ft 8 in. over couplers, with a gross weight of 4½ tons.

92 Improvised tank wagon (France)

As might be expected from a wine-making country accustomed to cast its products about in bulk, the French artillery railways utilised large casks as their liquid containers. No dimensions are available for this vehicle which was produced only in small numbers, to meet local demand, but the idea behind

it was not new. It was the custom of several continental main-line railways of the period to convey liquid in wagons consisting essentially of two or three huge casks on a normal underframe.

MORE ADVANCED PETROL TRACTORS (60-cm. gauge)

93 Deutz 4-wheeled tractor (German)

Thorough as always, the Germans had foreseen even before 1914 that light railways might need to enter the front-line areas and had made their arrangements. These included a large quantity of a standard 20-h.p. petrol-mechanical tractor designed by Deutz, an angular machine powered by a 2-cylinder water-cooled engine. Although cruder in concept than its later Allied equivalents, and still bearing traces of steam locomotive ancestry in its brass-capped exhaust 'chimney', it was none the less an efficient hauler over the well-laid German tracks. Drive was by jackshaft to the coupled wheels.

94 Baldwin petrol tractor (U.S.A.)

Almost as soon as the Germans, the French Artillery Railways Dept. realised that petrol tractors would be needed in quantity. French capacity was already occupied so they placed large orders in the United States for a petrol-mechanical machine designed and built by the Baldwin Locomotive Company. This had a 45 h.p., 4-cylinder water-cooled engine driving through a jackshaft onto coupled wheels; the drive shaft was positioned in front of the bonnet giving it an odd appearance and, like the Deutz it had a steam-locomotive pattern exhaust 'chimney'. These tractors had a reputation for jerkiness and harshness of operation but were used extensively by both French and Americans; the latter adopted them as standard when they entered the war.

95 Schneider 6-wheeled 0-6-0P tractor (France)

Standard 'home-built' tractor of the French artillery railways was the 6-coupled machine seen here. It was of Pechot design, with a degree of articulation in the axles and a typical Pechot cab. It was powered by a 4-cylinder water-cooled petrol engine developing 60 h.p., and driving through a four-speed gearbox onto a jackshaft. The machine was not really suitable for front-line work being designed specifically for moving heavy artillery pieces on the 60-cm. gauge fortress railways, and was utilised mainly in base areas.

96 Simplex 20-h.p. tractor (U.K.)

The British, when they finally took up light railways in a big way, were by far the largest users of petrol engined tractors, and their success was due almost entirely to the products of the Motor Rail & Tramcar Co. of Bedford —trade name 'Simplex'. This firm in turn owed its success to the Dixon Abbott gearbox invented by its founder and capable of giving smooth operation with two or three speeds in either direction; it almost entirely obviated the problems of jerkiness and low reverse gearing found in other transmissions of the period while with practice gear

changes could easily be made on the move. Even more fortunately, Mr Abbott had before the war seen German light railway preparations and had in anticipation designed a light 20-h.p. machine weighing only $2\frac{1}{2}$ tons in working order and powered by a 4-cylinder water-cooled engine driving through his patent gearbox. This historic design, shown here in detail, was at first rejected by Lord Kitchener in person as being 'not our way of working' but proved so versatile that it later became the maid of all work on W.D. light railways. It could haul two bogie wagons over good track and was notable for ruggedness and ease of maintenance; the frame was open and the engine covered only by a removable hood. Experiments were made with an armoured cab but it was not popular, the enginemen preferring freedom to leap off if shelled! The 20-h.p. Simplex served on all fronts throughout 1916–18, and over 500 were produced. The design continued in production for some years after the war and its direct successors have only recently been phased out.

97 Simplex 40 h.p. 'open' tractor (U.K.)

The light Simplex 20-h.p. tractors proved invaluable wherever they appeared but they had one severe disadvantage—their haulage power over the rickety track was often limited by adhesion to one bogie wagon. This was not so vital in the extreme front areas where a train of five wagons might be scheduled for five destinations, and thus composed of five separate 'tractor-wagon' groups, but it was a handicap further back.

When the Motor Rail Co. proposed

an enlarged version, therefore, the War Department was enthusiastic. The 'new' tractor was a more massive version of the old with plate frames instead of channel steel ones and with the driver mounted centrally. It had a 4-cylinder water-cooled engine of 40 h.p. and the ends were protected by heavy, armoured steel curved shields which also acted as ballast weights; further weights were bolted to the frames, bringing adhesion weight up to 6 tons which was still within the permitted axle-loading for 20 lb/yd rail. A pillar roof protected the driver.

98 Simplex 40 h.p. 'protected' tractor (U.K.)

In certain exposed areas, trains were exposed to sniper fire and a number of the 40-h.p. tractors were built with driver protection. This comprised armoured side doors to the cab, and a lowered roof provided with steel 'visors' at sides and ends to enable the driver to look out. When not needed, the doors could be hooked back to provide ventilation to what must have been a hot airless and very noisy steel box! Over 120 of these machines were supplied.

99/101 Petrol-electric tractors (U.K.)

Undoubtedly one of the most interesting 60-cm. gauge motive power units to come out of World War One was the British War Department design for a 4-wheeled petrol-electric tractor. This had its origin in the realisation that steam locomotives were too conspicuous for working up to the front lines and someone had the bright idea of electrify-

ing the forward area lines with overhead pick-up. The project even got so far as to be included in the main outline order programme for 1916–17 but in its original form was then quietly dropped. Possibly someone with front-line experience realised the difficulties of maintaining such equipment under constant shellfire; possibly the Simplex petrol-mechanicals were already proving their worth. In either case the overhead idea was put into abeyance but the original order for 200 electric locomotives was completed—as petrol electric tractors.

These were fascinating machines in their own right. It seems likely that the War Office was to some extent hedging its bets since the machines were designed for not a dual but a triple purpose role. Each order was strictly not for 100 machines but for 50 pairs, deliberately designed to work as straight electric double locomotives if the need arose. Thus the electric motors could be driven direct from a suitable current supply, one of each pair was fitted with electrical connections and socket to take a trolley pole, and the generators could be connected in parallel via a built-in junction box. In the event these provisions were never used. The machines materialised with 45–55-h.p. petrol engines driving the electrical equipment; the design was by British Westinghouse Ltd. who were main contractors for 100 locomotives, the other 100 being built by Dick Kerr at Kilmarnock.

They were equipped with armour shuttering to cover the cab and radiator for front-line work, although this was rarely used in practice and also had provision for starting the petrol engine via another unit's generator—a wise move since it was easy to do oneself an injury trying to 'swing' the big engine by hand.

The main identification differences were that the Dick Kerr machines, seen in Plate 100 as a pair, had louvered bonnet sides, the Westinghouse ones (Plate 99) had panelled sides. Each unit, with its two 22·5-h.p. motors, could pull three or four bogie wagons in service and could also act as a mobile generating station for powering workshops—a feature not found on any equivalent tractors elsewhere. The 'PE's' were in general coveted by their 'owners' since they were strong and flexible in operation; their usefulness was limited only by a low top speed and the reputation of some for stubbornness.

Main dimensions were: loaded weight 8 tons; 55-h.p. 4-cylinder water-cooled petrol engine; driving two 22·5-h.p. electric motors via a 30-kW. generator set at 500 V.

ARMOURED TRACTORS
(60-cm. gauge)

A specialised development of petrol-engined motive power was the fully armoured tractor—virtually a small, unarmed tank on rails—which was produced in small quantities for use in very exposed areas. It was not popular in service, being almost unbearable for its driver and very heavy to heave back on the track when it derailed.

102 Decauville-Crochat petrol-electric tractor (France)

The French artillery railways had such machines in service in the fortified areas even before the war; their requirement was logical since the outlying forts had

to be supplied under fire. The 'standard' armoured tractor was a bogie, petrol-electric machine on the Crochat system —later used for a number of railcars. This had a transversely-mounted 4-cylinder water-cooled petrol engine driving electric motors through a generator, the petrol engine occupying one end of the body and the generator the other. Characteristic of all Crochat machines was the side-mounted cooling fan drawing its air through a circular, gauze-covered porthole. The armoured protecting cover for this can be seen at the rear end by the soldier. Entry was via a two-part 'stable-door' placed centrally on each side.

103 Simplex 40-h.p. armoured tractor (U.K.)

The British contribution was a modification of the ubiquitous Simplex petrol-mechanical, four-wheeled tractor, in this case the 40 h.p. version. This really did look like a miniature tank, being totally enclosed with only small vision slits for the driver and was reputedly appallingly hot and noisy to drive. The additional armour added nearly a ton to the all-up weight bringing it, with driver to 7·2 tons (Simplex weights, rather quaintly, always included a hypothetical 12-stone driver). Only 27 were put into service.

104/105 American armoured tractors

The Americans inevitably decided to go one better and produced complete armoured trains at least in prototype form. There is little information on these which so far as is known never entered service on the Western Front. Plate 104 shows a rather rakish and long petrol locomotive by Hall-Scott, apparently with two motors. Plate 105 is an obvious prototype of an oil-electric machine officially termed an 'armoured motor car'. Like the Hall-Scott it is fitted with an automatic coupler, and even the bogies have armoured 'skirts'.

MOTOR AMBULANCE TROLLEYS

106/109 **Drewry 'B' type motor ambulance trolleys** (U.K.)

Final refinement of the narrow gauge military ambulance vehicle was the motorised trolley with special body-work. This was not produced in great numbers by any of the combatants but *was* used on the so-called 'colonial' fronts where narrow gauge railways often acted as lines of communication; they were, therefore, often quite long. A total of 25 such cars was built for the British operations in Mesopotamia and these are described below.

106 **Drewry 'B' type trolley chassis**

Basis of the cars was the Drewry Car Co.'s standard 'B' type motor trolley chassis designed to be adaptable to all gauges. These were actually built by Drewry's subsidiary, Baguley Cars Ltd., and were typical of a pattern adopted by both British and continental manu-facturers. The chassis consisted of a straightforward metal underframe about 16 ft long, with a wheelbase of 7 ft. The 4-cylinder Baguley petrol engine de-veloping 20 h.p. was mounted at one end under a pair of transverse seats and drove onto one axle. It was water-cooled, horizontal tube radiators being

fitted to both ends of the car, and dup-licate sets of driver's controls were provided though in common with tram-car practice the actual operating levers had to be transferred when the driver changed ends. Unusually the handbrakes were of car-type lever pattern and not handwheels. The cars had three-speed gearboxes with reversing box and maxi-mum speed was about 35 m.p.h.

107 **Motor trolley in use for stretcher patients**

The body comprised a central 'compart-ment' with a driver's platform at each end. It was designed with a central space giving access to the driving platforms via a door in the middle of each end bulkhead, and was fitted to take two stretchers at each side. An attendant could therefore service the stretcher cases while the car was moving and a seat was provided for him against one end-bulkhead. Alternatively, the stretchers could be removed, the plat-forms holding the upper ones folded into the roof, and a canvas seat for six lightly wounded men could be erected; this normally was kept folded down to form the car floor.

108 **Motor trolley ready for running**

To protect the patients from rain, wind and sand the cars were equipped with full length canvas side-curtains which could be let down to enclose the body. These were normally furled under the roof eaves, and bore the red cross on a white background. The remainder of the curtains and the vehicle bodywork were coloured khaki in accordance with normal military practice.

109 Drewry passenger motor trolley

Not specifically an ambulance vehicle, but equally typical of the period was the Drewry trolley pictured here for use on the 4 ft 8½ in. gauge. This pattern of vehicle, with its swing-over seats, its motor under the seat boxes and its end radiators, hardly varied over the years, though presumably improvements were constantly being made to the motors and mechanical parts. Cars of this type were used widely for inspection and permanent way purposes by all armies. This particular one was built for Mesopotamia and is a six-seater; 10 ft 4 in. long with a wheelbase of 5 ft 5 in.

METRE GAUGE ROLLING-STOCK

110 Metre gauge 4-wheeled wagon (U.K. for Belgium)

Besides specialised narrow-gauge railways, both sides in World War One also utilised existing narrow gauge local railways where these existed. The Germans, Austrians and French normally used the existing stock, supplementing it as required with further equipment commandeered from local railways in their own countries outside the fighting zone. Great Britain had never possessed a rational system of secondary railways, and certainly had none on the metre gauge. Her positions in the north around Ypres and the Belgian coast, however, included big segments of the Belgian National Secondary Railways Co. (Societé Nationale des Chemins de Fer Vicinaux), a concern operating almost entirely on the metre gauge. The War Department had therefore to provide 50 train locomotives of standard Belgian pattern and, in addition, no less than 1200 wagons. These were mainly 4-wheeled 10-ton open wagons of a type standardised by the S.N.C.V. and fitted with normal S.N.C.V. draw gear. A number were fitted with brakesman's perches as shown here.

111 Metre gauge refrigerator van

The Middle East Fronts included considerable mileage of metre gauge railways, especially in Mesopotamia. Most stock for these lines was commandeered from Indian lines but some specialist vehicles were built in England. They included these substantial bogie refrigerator cars built to order Mesrail 7 as early as autumn 1916 and taring 17 tons 16 cwt. It will be seen that, in contrast to the light equipment used in France and Belgium, these lines were built as long-distance systems to a high standard. The vehicles were supplied by Leeds Forge Co.

WORKSHOP TRAINS (60-cm. gauge, U.K.)

Once the British decided to take light railways seriously they were in many ways the most inventive of the combatants in World War One. One example was the series of complete mobile workshop trains built for the W.D. light railways early in 1918 by the Gloucester Carriage & Wagon Co. Each train was specified to be capable of carrying out running repairs to equipment in the field and was composed of six vehicles.

112 Office van for workshop train (U.K.)

This provided quarters for the senior officer in charge of the train and his assistants. It was fully equipped, the senior officer even having an electric radiator run off the train's generator system and was, like all the other vehicles, mounted on a standard 'D' class underframe.

113 Tool and stores wagon

Included in the train were one or more ordinary bogie vans with side-opening doors and equipped with racks for tools, lockers for stores and two small swivel cranes or derricks. They were arranged so that the interior also provided working space for artificers engaged on small jobs and an awning could be stretched over the opened doors to provide a kind of porch.

114/115 Machinery wagon, closed and open

The other three vehicles in the train were machine wagons. They had van bodies with the sides designed to open up to provide increased working space. Each side was in three sections and each section was split into an upper and lower flap. The lower flap dropped down to become a working floor, suspended on chains (though they were usually supplemented by baulks of wood); the upper one was raised horizontally to form a roof or canopy that could in turn be supplemented by tarpaulin awnings. Two of these vehicles contained machine tools comprising grindstones, drills, a shaping machine and a 6-in. lathe, driven from overhead shafting. The third was a generator car which provided power to light and heat the train besides powering the machinery. The plant consisted of two 15–20-amp. Aster petrol engines driving a 10-kW. dynamo and was completely self-contained, water and petrol tanks being provided in the car.

An interesting feature of the trains was that the two workshop cars could be used individually away from their parent train, connections being provided so that they could take power from a petrol electric tractor (Plate 99). The trains were intended for use away from established depots—for example in the case of a rapid advance—but were also used as auxiliary base workshops.

116 60-cm. gauge railway in abandoned village

World War One saw one marked change in the relationship of railways and war. Before 1914, railways might have been *at* war but rarely were *in* it. True the railway acting as a line of communication occasionally got tangled up with the fighting through accident or enemy infiltration. It even got torn up in places. Yet basically earlier wars were wars of movements and the railways normally operated behind advancing or retreating lines largely over existing civilian tracks. The most that was done was to build the occasional military feeder railway.

In 1914 the war of movement suddenly stopped, and stopped arbitrarily wherever the armies halted each other. Since the fighting was for once in a populous region, whole farms, villages and, later, even towns such as Albert and Ypres found themselves deserted and caught in the battle zone. Standard gauge railheads became static and a network of light narrow gauge feeders penetrated the battle zone. The railway came into the war as a daily part of its life, a scene typified by this ammunition train wandering through a wrecked village almost in the front line. For probably the first time, such railways had to be operated under the threat of constant shelling in forward areas. Their track ballast and the rough roads by which they ran, were even composed at times of the rubble of the villages they helped the guns to destroy. To cope with this new railway operating organisations expanded on both sides of the line. The Germans, and in Italy the Austrians, ran them as railways, with proper procedures and even system names. The British, and to a lesser extent the French and Americans were more flexible, evolving new methods and new material to meet the new situations. This British train, with its internal combustion engined tractor to help escape observation, and its high capacity bogie vehicles each of which could carry the load of an ordinary standard gauge 10-ton wagon, marks the new approach; its background is symbolic of the change in attitude.

LIGHT RAILWAY LOADS (60-cm. gauge)

One of the more surprising things about the tactical 'field' railways that sprung up during World War One was their versatility. They could—and did—carry almost everything since the overall bogie wagon capacity of about 10 tons was usually more than sufficient. Indeed the only cargo likely to overtax a wagon,

and thus lead to empty space in it, was the ammunition for medium and heavy artillery. In this case, 10 tons of shell, distributed, normally took up only about two-thirds of the available floor space; otherwise the load was restricted only by cubic capacity.

It was for this reason that the French and British designed well-wagon variants of their standard vehicles. The plates show the most efficient examples, the British 'E' class (sided) and 'F' class (flat with stanchions) which had many parts interchangeable with their 'D' class equivalent. It will be noticed that, as in the French design, the vehicle was not a true well-wagon with cranked underframe, but simply had the centre portion between bogies dropped to form a stout box. This had the dual advantage of lowering the centre of gravity when light loads were carried and of allowing the main underframe solebars to be unbroken from end to end. The latter feature retained the structural strength of the original standard design without a weight penalty but did hamper unloading of small heavy items (e.g. cases of small arms ammunition)—hence the retention of the standard non-well-wagon for many purposes. The plates show typical loads carried by the light railways and for which well-vehicles were suited.

117 'E' class wagon loaded with heavy shells

The unbroken underframe girders made it quite possible to carry a full load of heavy shells which were normally stacked over the bogies in any case; the positioning made a wagon more stable and avoided placing too much strain on the underframe centre. The centre 'well' of an 'E' class came in very useful for the odd roll of barbed wire and other light battery stores that might be needed.

118 'F' class well-wagon with forage

A fairly common load for the light railways was horse and mule fodder. In the case of this light load, the extra cubic capacity of a well-wagon was extremely useful, and the stanchioned variety more convenient than a sided one which had only one door each side.

119 'E' class wagon with wreckage (aircraft)

Crashed aircraft were uncommon loads, though occasionally conveyed, but the drawing symbolises all the salvage that made up a good part of light railway traffic especially during the aftermath of an offensive.

120 'D' class wagon with ballast

Lastly for comparison, this shows a standard non-well-wagon carrying a load for which a flat floor and drop sides throughout were essential. Almost a quarter of light railways traffic was constructional, either ballast and track material for themselves or road-making material as shown here.

ROLLING-STOCK JIGSAWS (60-cm. gauge)

One of the most dearly loved concepts of the military railway designers was the all-purpose vehicle. The French started it with their '40 or 50 hommes, 8 chevaux'

goods vans on the standard gauge (Plate 151). The British, in particular, took up the idea on the 60-cm. gauge with what might almost be called universal pack-away wagons.

121/122 'A' class 4-wheeled wagon (U.K.)

The very first 'standard' 60-gauge vehicle for W.D. light railways was the 'A' class wagon introduced late in 1915. This was a small 4-wheeled vehicle, 7 ft 4½ in. long by 4 ft wide (over body), having sprung axleboxes, proper centre buffer-couplers and a ratchet brake. It was designed for either locomotive or mule haulage, side chains or staples being provided for affixing the swingletrees of mule teams, and was essentially a high sided wagon of normal pattern. The sides, however, were hinged to fold flat across the wagon floor and the ends had pivoting hinges to enable them to be raised slightly and then folded down on top of the flattened sides. The vehicle could thus become a rather thick-floored flat wagon (Plate 122) and for this role it was equipped with four corner sockets each holding a massive stanchion. Three ring bolts were provided on each side of the solebar for securing loads. The wagons, of which two variants existed, tared either 17 cwt or 18 cwt and had a disposable load of about 3½ tons.

123/124 'P' class 4-wheeled wagon (U.K.)

In some ways a rather more sophisticated return to the 'A' class was the 'P' class wagon produced by the British towards the end of the war. Like the 'A' class it was 4-wheeled, with sprung axleboxes and a ratchet brake, but there the comparison ended. The 'P' class was especially designed for transfer work between W.D. light railways and the light trench tramways. It therefore was capable of locomotive or tractor haulage on suitable track, but also had an axle-load and capacity (1 ton) suitable for man haulage over the light 9 lb/yd rails of the forward area tramways. Its bodywork was even more versatile than that of the 'A' class. Basically a flat wagon, it could quickly be fitted with barred ends dropping into stanchion sockets and capable of supporting two tiers of stretchers. For dual purpose work these could be supplemented by hinged sides, latticed for lightness, which could be either folded down on to the floor or removed entirely when needed. As a final variant the 'stretcher' ends could be quickly replaced by latticed ones matching the sides. Any combination of these variations was possible! Wagon length over solebars was 6 ft 6 in.; width 4 ft.

125/126 'B' and 'C' class wagons (U.K.)

The next British designs were even more ingenious—probably too much so since subsequent standard wagons became simpler and more specialised. These wagons were the 'B' class 4-wheelers and the 'C' class bogie vehicles both introduced early in 1916. As can be seen from the plates they were developments of the earlier theme. Each vehicle was basically a flat wagon on to which side and end panels could be either socketed or hinged. The new feature was that the 'B' class wagon was exactly half the length of a 'C' class which in turn had each of its sides made up from two strongly braced panels. Both these and the wagon ends were therefore standardised between the classes as was most of the running gear—wheels and axleboxes in particular. The idea was obviously to produce wagons capable of easy cannibalisation in case of damage by enemy fire but it would appear that the ease with which detachable items could be dumped and lost outweighed the advantages. Certainly later vehicles had their bits and pieces firmly attached.

127/128 Standard well-wagons (France)

The French artillery railways also had their moments of ingenuity. They did have a standard sided bogie wagon but they also had, especially for carriage of fodder and shells, the pattern of vehicle shown here. This was basically a heavy, plate-framed flat wagon with a central well to give a low centre of gravity when carrying heavy ammunition. It was fitted with removable stanchions at sides and ends, had ring bolts fixed along each side of the frame and could be either locomotive or mule-hauled. Its interest lay in the fact that the complete underframe-body shell was built in one piece and could simply be lifted bodily off the bogies. These in turn were capable of acting as independent units. Fitted with bolsters revolving on the bogie pivot ring and linked by a long cylindrical tie bar, they immediately became a timber wagon capable of carrying wood beams, rails or other long objects. A kit as supplied by the manufacturers consisted of one body, one bolster, one pole and two bogies, each of the latter having a pillar hand-brake. Presumably only one bolster was supplied because it was thought unlikely that more than half the wagons supplied would be used in this mode at any one time!

129 'F' class well-wagon (U.K.)

The British equivalent to the French wagon described in Plate 127 was the 'F' class vehicle, one of a series of standard wagons produced for the 1916 programme. This fulfilled much the same function, in carrying light but bulky loads but was not so versatile. It was a nominal 10-tonner, with a body length of 17 ft 8½ in. and its main feature was the 'well' or, rather, lidless box, that occupied the centre portion. This was not a true well since the underframe solebars were unbroken but it did provide a low-centre of gravity and useful extra space when carrying light loads such as fodder. Otherwise the vehicle was a normal flat wagon with detachable wooden stanchions at side and ends, these fitting into metal sockets on the underframe. All major parts were interchangeable with the other standard underframes of classes 'D', 'E' and 'H'. The vehicle was, in common with them, a very efficient load carrier having a tare weight of only 2 tons 2 cwt., as against a disposable load of 9 tons 18 cwt.

SPECIAL VEHICLES for 60-cm. GAUGE

Light railways were mainly intended for moving material, and when people had to be moved it was usually in bulk—in the manner shown in Plate 153. Even smaller parties just dumped their gear in wagons and climbed aboard. Senior (*very* senior) personnel, however, were another matter and most systems of any size eventually scraped together one or two presentable vehicles at least.

130 V.I.P. coach of British 2nd Army (1918)

The British used staff cars. Yet every one of the Army light railways at one time or another fabricated some form of coach in their own workshops for use by very senior officers on tours of inspection; most also used them for more mundane purposes. 3rd Army for example had what was said to be a very fine glazed coach of which no picture survives. When it was not toting the generals about, it formed the base depot ration train. Perhaps the most famous was the 2nd Army vehicle shown here. Obviously formed from an ordinary 'D' class wagon with a hut at one end and a corrugated-iron roof covering an observation verandah at the other, it was relatively crude but was used on one occasion by H.M. the King. It thus attained photographic immortality.

131 Office coach, Canadian Corps (1917)

The Canadians claimed that they inspired the whole of W.D. Light Railways (false) and built most of the central section (true). In their inimitable style they provided themselves with this very sophisticated vehicle. The 'standard' bogie underframe was just recognisable but the entirely new body with its transatlantic-pattern domed roof was a work of art. Outside it was— rather superfluously—painted in a dazzle camouflage pattern more often used to deceive U-boats on the high seas. Inside it was a very efficient office, with desk, filing equipment and a splendid cast-iron stove. The Canadian Corps was very proud of it.

132 Metal-bodied tip truck for ballast (all armies)

All the warring nations used their military light railway systems for mainly domestic purposes as well as for war-like ones. In particular they carried much ballast and roadstone both for their own use and for that of other units. To carry out this task efficiently they were equipped with side tipping wagons of the normal industrial pattern. The most common was the 'V'-shaped metal 'skip' of either 18 or 27 cu. feet—or their continental equivalents—which was virtually an international design. Orenstein & Koppel in Germany, Robert Hudson in Britain, Decauville in France all turned out essentially similar vehicles in which the 'V'-shaped body had inherent instability and was simply located by two pins and a retaining stop at each side. When a stop was pulled out, the body automatically tipped to the appropriate side and deposited its load. A typical wagon had a wheelbase of 1 ft 10 in. with a wheel diameter of only 12 in., and was just over 7 ft long over frame ends.

133 American tip truck (U.S.A.)

This plate shows an American variant of the same type of wagon. It is, if anything, even more stubby in appearance but is included here mainly to show the large white lettering favoured by the U.S. Army and to show the tapered end bucket that was fitted to some vehicles. Dimensions are similar to those of the truck above.

134 American pattern tip truck, upright and tipped (U.S.A. for U.K.)

During 1916, the British manufacturing capacity appeared likely to be fully occupied for some months to come, but there was an urgent need for tipping wagons. A trial order was therefore placed with an American firm, the Western Wheeled Scraper Co., which specialised in contractor's equipment. Their standard 60-cm. gauge tipper was of a type largely obsolete in Britain because of its needless complication. It consisted of a metal underframe with a rectangular oak-planked body mounted above it on three in-line pivots. The body had side-doors, pivoted at the top and was kept in place by chains leading down to the underframe, one at each corner. This body was inherently unbalanced and was tipped simply by releasing the chains on one side when it swung over. The door also swung open and released the load. The wagons had a capacity of 40 cu. ft and a wheelbase of 2 ft 10 in. They proved acceptable but British firms proved able to meet all demands so no more were ordered. They were put into service as W.D.L.R. Class L.

Carrying howitzers on trucks (U.K.)

Curiously, although the French Government Artillery Railways were set up specifically to supply artillery needs, it was the British who made most imaginative use of light railways to cart field guns around. Whole batteries, up to and including even 4·7-in. naval guns, were moved from one location to another in this way thus saving considerable time and trouble; after all movement by road not only cuttered up the roads but often involved a long haul through mud. The light railways, on the other hand, almost by definition could deliver guns right to the battery position; they were usually already in place to deal with ammunition supply. On at least one section of the front there was even a 'flying column' of 18-pounders which would move rapidly to a given position, carry out a brisk shelling and then be back on its rail trucks and away before the enemy could pin-point them and retaliate. These views show how a 6-in. howitzer was loaded for rail-transport.

135 Modified bogie well-wagon

There were many variants of gun wagons, but the 'usual' one was an 'F' class well-wagon (Plate 129) with its stanchions removed and two steel troughs slung outboard of the wagon solebars and supported by girders or beams across the body. When it was desired to load a gun, this was backed into a suitable position and massive detachable ramps were placed in position at one end, straddling the rail track.

136 Loading howitzer via ramps

The gun was then moved up to these barrel first, and hauled up onto the wagon by brute force, the wheels running in the troughs which were broad enough to accommodate most patterns of field artillery—haulage could be

either by man-power or by the locomotive moving away and pulling the gun up after it.

137 Howitzer on wagon

Once on the wagon, the gun was supported in 'firing position' with the tail spade projecting over one bogie. It will be noticed that the wheel troughs normally extended only about three-quarters of the way along the wagon, since the gun barrel projected over the remainder. They were supported both above and below by massive beams.

138 Howitzer and limber in travelling position

Final act of loading was to run the limber up onto the wagon, resting on the gun tail. This was possible with the 6-in. howitzer and other low slung weapons, although certain high-trailed guns had to have their limbers carried separately. The loading ramps were then detached and stowed on the wagon body alongside the gun trail and the vehicle was ready to depart. Complete trains of these wagons were hauled, special long coupling bars being provided where the guns projected too far over the ends of the wagons.

TRANSPORTING TANKS BY RAIL
(Standard Gauge)

139/142 One big difficulty solved by the Transportation Branch of the Mechanical Warfare Department was the carriage of tanks (the armoured fighting vehicle variety) from their manufacturers to the forward stores parks. The heaviest tanks

weighed nearly 35 tons and this, com-
bined with their height which fouled the
normal loading gauge, meant that no
standard wagons could do the job. The
outcome, designed and produced extremely rapidly in early 1917 was the
special R(ailway) E(xecutive) C(ommit-
tee) Tank carrier or Rectank wagon of
which some 787 were eventually built.
As can be seen from Plate 139, this was a
long, low bogie wagon, some 37 ft 2 in.
long and with a platform height above
rail of only 3 ft 6½ in.; as is evidenced
by its tare weight of some 15½ tons,
the wagon underframe was massively
strengthened to take the concentrated
weight of a tank between the bogies
when being loaded from the side (Plates
139/140). Normal procedure was to run
the tank on broadside on, under its own
power and then manipulate its track
steering to slow it into travelling position. Once in position the tank was
secured fore and aft by massive chains.

There was, however, an alternative
loading method, when a side ramp was
not available. This was to load the
vehicle over the slightly raised end and
for this purpose the wagons were fitted
at each end with a pair of heavy screw
jacks (Plate 141). These could be lowered
to take the strain off the appropriate
bogie, the bogie bolsters being specially
strengthened in addition. An interesting
if rather useless discovery during trials
was that careful positioning of a tank
on the wagon end acted as a counter-
balance to the remainder of the underframe which would pivot freely round
the affected bogie! The plates show the
process of loading from the side, with a
tank nosing onto the wagon (Plate 139);
partially swing round (Plate 140) and in
travelling position (Plate 141/42).

TRANSPORTING TANKS IN THE FIELD

The transportation of tanks from England to France was, of course, only a
small part of the total operation. It was
often necessary to move tanks considerable distances in and behind the battle
zones either to bring out captured or
disabled vehicles, or to move up complete squadrons of vehicles for an im-
pending attack. Since efficient road-
transporter vehicles had not yet been
developed, the tanks had to be moved
either by rail or on their own tracks;
the latter expedient was used as little as
possible owing to the inherent unreli-
ability of these early mechanical mon-
sters. There was therefore always a need
for large quantities of wagons and for
some means of loading and unloading in
primitive conditions.

143/144 Ramp wagon for loading tanks

Means of unloading where no loading
banks existed was provided by use of
special ramp wagons delivered in the
spring of 1918. These were built by the
little known firm of Stableford and Co.
of Coalville, and were basically long-
wheelbase (12 ft 8 in.) flat wagons with
massive channel steel solebars and cross
members to the underframe. One pair of
wheels on its axle was detachable as a
unit complete with axlebox; removal
being effected by means of a pillar screw-
jack which could lift the entire underframe and enable the wheels to be
unbolted and run out from underneath
the wagon. The other end was equipped
with a pair of strong steel-channel
girder supports which were packed up
on sleepers to make a firm ramp.

145 Loading tanks via a ramp wagon

The plate shows how tanks were loaded on to a train of bogie wagons. The procedure was somewhat similar to the present-day one of loading cars on to a car carrying train. Each tank simply crawled up the ramp wagon which was positioned end-on to a train of wagons and fitted with hardwood cleats to give the tracks something to grip. The receiving wagons were positioned with all screw jacks lowered on to steeper packing and taking the weight, so that each tank simply drove gingerly along the train to its appointed wagon. Most common receiving vehicles were of course the standard RecTank wagons as seen here, often equipped with extra jacks under the centre part of the underframe. It will be noted that, where loading gauge restrictions permitted, tanks about to take part in an operation were often transported in battle condition. These British Mk. IVs are carrying fascines for bridging trenches and other small obstacles.

146 Stableford 40-ton well-wagon with captured tanks

The demand for tank carrying vehicles led to other wagons than the RecTank being employed in small numbers. One specially designed wagon was the 40-ton well-wagon shown here. This was a massively-framed wagon built in small quantities by Stableford & Co. in spring and summer of 1918 to cope with the increasing weight and size of armoured vehicles—hence the well, to ease loading gauge problems. It had a wood plank decking to give grip to tank tracks and could be either side or end-loaded. As with the RecTank, heavy screw jacks were provided at either end and at each end of the well. This particular example is pictured carrying a German ATV tank captured during the British offensives of summer 1918.

147 Ex-GWR Macaw bogie wagon with Renault tanks

Civilian bogie wagons were pressed into service at times especially for carrying lighter armoured vehicles. This shows an ex GWR Macaw wagon of the Woolmer Instructional Military Railway (later replaced by the Longmoor Military Railway) carrying two light French Renault tanks; these were light enough even to be carried on the 60-cm. gauge and were normally loaded either side-on or by crane. It was normal practice in the field for available railway wagons to be used to carry any Allied vehicles as required.

RAIL-BORNE CRANE

148 35-ton breakdown crane (U.K.)

War conditions on railways inevitably lead to an increase in derailments and, hence, the need for efficient rescue equipment. For most of World War One, the British War Department was dependent on second-hand breakdown cranes or on equipment borrowed from the British main line railways. It was not until 1918 that a standard 35-ton crane was produced for the Transportation Department by Stothert and Pitt Ltd. This was a girder-jib steam crane mounted on one 6-wheeled and one

4-wheeled bogie, and fitted with the usual sponson outriggers for stability when working. It normally ran with two standard match-wagons, a long-wheelbase 4-wheeler to carry the jib and a low-sided bogie wagon for stores and equipment. The crane was capable of the heaviest tasks envisaged by the R.O.D. and could easily lift a normal 0-6-0 goods locomotive when using the appropriate yoke.

STANDARD GAUGE SHUNTING LOCOMOTIVES

149 **Baldwin 2-6-2ST** (U.S.A. for U.K.)

Among the smaller locomotive types ordered for the R.O.D. standard gauge lines in France was this massive looking 2-6-2 saddle-tank. Its character comes partly from the big saddle-tank with its steam dome and two-sandboxes dwarfing the cab, but the boiler was also large for a locomotive of this nature. It appears to have been intended for heavy yard switching and for handling trains over portions of route where no turning facilities were available. One hundred were ordered from the ever prolific Baldwin locomotive works in May, 1917 under the R.O.D. serials 1501–1600 but there is some doubt as to whether more than 75 were ever delivered.

150 **Baldwin 0-6-0T** (U.S.A. for U.K.)

More like the normal shunting-engines were 50 0-6-0 side-tank locomotives delivered from Baldwins in the winter of

1917–18. Unusual features for American locomotives included the British-pattern cab with rear coal bunker and what appears to be a crude feed-water heater. The locomotives were intended for yard and dock shunting, as witness the twin sandboxes and the bell; this was an obligatory fitting on French railways for locomotives likely to work alongside or over roads. R.O.D. running numbers were in the 651–700 series.

MOVING MEN BY RAIL

Officers had special coaches; the rank and file got rougher treatment although even the roughest was far preferable to having to march for miles and miles.

151 **The 'Blighty' train**

Perhaps one of the major memories for many troops was the 'Blighty' train, taking them to the ports on leave, or as wounded; and, not quite such a pleasant memory, its equivalent conveying them to the front. This was usually composed of the oldest and most ramshackle vehicles available and especially in the early days of the war when slogans were rife. These often got covered with scrawled remarks. No doubt the long-suffering railways regarded them in much the same light as present day concerns regard football match 'specials', and budgeted accordingly.

152 **50 hommes, 8 chevaux**

As the war went on, even elderly carriages became a luxury. It was probably the French, that logical race, who first hit on the idea of the 'dual-purpose' van, and not only calculated that one horse took up the space occupied by five men, but said so on the loading instructions. They saw nothing odd in it; after all the equivalent tradition of 'fourth class' for natives in both British and French colonies was longstanding and what were the military but a species of native? The truck inscription which led to so many wry jokes was merely a sensible administrative advice to stop the vehicle being overloaded and ensure that its occupants had enough fresh air; the grilled air vents, coverable by hinged flaps in inclement weather, were standard for such trucks.

153 Moving men on the 60-cm. gauge

The light railways on both sides were even more basic in their transportation. They simply cleared the ammunition or the salvage out of trucks and filled them up with men. It was in any case an act of disinterested kindness on their part to carry people in bulk since the Poor Bloody Infantry were supposed to march the five odd miles to or from base when relieving each other in the front line. In such circumstances nobody objected to crowding and discomfort and in the later stages of the war trains like this became common. At least on the British Light Railways, all the operating districts did their best to respond to the requests and it was not unknown for a complete regiment (two battalions) to be moved in a few hours by a succession of trains. As for the men and their officers, on a cold wet night with the roads ankle deep in mud, even forty to a wagon was sheer luxury.

154 Ambulance wagons for the 60-cm. gauge

One of the most common reasons for moving men at all by rail, especially near the front line, was also one of the most tragic; seriously wounded soldiers had to be conveyed to the rear with as little further harm as possible. The work of the numerous standard gauge hospital trains is famous but it may not be so well known that even the light railways had their ambulance trains. The British ones were typical examples.

First British use of ambulance vehicles was on the lines of communication specifically at a series of base hospitals on the Trouville Plateau which were reached over a light railway some $5\frac{1}{2}$ miles in length. For these a series of large covered vans was built, based on a lengthened and widened bogie wagon chassis.

These vans were officially dual purpose vehicles, being convertible for the carriage of goods. They were fitted to carry nine stretchers in tiers of three, one tier being faced by a longitudinal seat for walking wounded, and had a centre corridor with access through sliding or hinged double doors at each side. In addition narrow-end doors allowed attendants to pass through the train while in motion. These vans were later used also in rear areas on the front-line railway system and several have survived.

Much more common on the British side, however, were the numerous conversions of standard bogie wagons to the ambulance role. As can be seen both the 'D' and 'E' series were thus utilised, a standard 'conversion kits' being provided which included stretchers, racks and a framed tarpaulin 'roof' with side and end flaps; up to twelve stretchers could be accommodated, though six were more usual. These wagons were a great improvement on the former methods of perching stretchers on any available vehicle but were not by any means perfect; with the screens down and a full load the atmosphere inside must have been stifling and loading was not easy. In this respect the 'D' class was favoured since it had full length drop doors while the 'E' class had only a central door; on the other hand the well on an 'E' class enabled the attendant to stand upright within the wagon.

ARMOURED TRAIN 1918-style

155/156 **Czech-built armoured trolley** (*c.* 1918)

Very little is known about this interesting vehicle, which is illustrated here to show a development just beginning to take effect at the end of World War One. It was built by Skoda Ltd. and was officially termed by the German Army an 'armoured trolley' (Panzerdraisine). Its stated purpose was to reconnoitre over railways destroyed or damaged by the enemy and to act as a protector for engineers restoring them—a sort of one car equivalent to the British armoured train of the South African War. Armament was two machine guns in a revolving turret and the armour was obviously intended to stop only small-arms fire and shrapnel splinters. The car was 3·5 m. long and 1·7 m. wide, and was designed for standard gauge. Like most trolleys it could not be marshalled into a train but a coupling pin and bar was provided so that it could be towed in an emergency. It was definitely an armoured rail trolley, not an armoured car on rails and a slightly updated version was indeed used by the Germans in World War Two.

INDEX